Assessing Educational Outcomes

Peter T. Ewell, *Editor*

NEW DIRECTIONS FOR INSTITUTIONAL RESEARCH

Sponsored by the Association for Institutional Research

PATRICK T. TERENZINI, *Editor in Chief*
MARVIN W. PETERSON, *Associate Editor*

Number 47, September 1985

Jossey-Bass Inc., Publishers
San Francisco • London

Peter T. Ewell (Ed.).
Assessing Educational Outcomes.
New Directions for Institutional Research, no. 47.
San Francisco: Jossey-Bass, 1985

New Directions for Institutional Research
Patrick T. Terenzini, *Editor-in-Chief*
Marvin W. Peterson, *Associate Editor*
Copyright © 1985 by Jossey-Bass Inc., Publishers
and
Jossey-Bass Limited

New Directions for Institutional Research (publication number
USPS 098-830) is published quarterly by Jossey-Bass Inc., Publishers, and
is sponsored by the Association for Institutional Research. The volume
and issue numbers above are included for the convenience of libraries.
Second-class postage rates paid at San Francisco, California, and at
additional mailing offices.

Correspondence:
Subscriptions, single-issue orders, change of address notices, undelivered
copies, and other correspondence should be sent to Subscriptions,
Jossey-Bass Inc., Publishers, 433 California Street, San Francisco,
California 94104.

Editorial correspondence should be sent to the Editor-in-Chief, Marvin W.
Peterson, Center for the Study of Higher Education, University of
Michigan, Ann Arbor, Michigan 48109, or Patrick T. Terenzini, Office of
Institutional Research, SUNY, Albany, New York 12222.

Library of Congress Catalog Card Number 85-60832

International Standard Serial Number ISSN 0271-0579

International Standard Book Number ISBN 87589-753-3

Cover art by WILLI BAUM

Manufactured in the United States of America

Ordering Information

The paperback sourcebooks listed below are published quarterly and can be ordered either by subscription or single-copy.

Subscriptions cost $40.00 per year for institutions, agencies, and libraries. Individuals can subscribe at the special rate of $30.00 per year *if payment is by personal check.* (Note that the full rate of $40.00 applied if payment is by institutional check, even if the subscription is designated for an individual.) Standing orders are accepted.

Single copies are available at $9.95 when payment accompanies order, and *all single-copy orders under $25.00 must include payment.* (California, New Jersey, New York, and Washington, D.C., residents please include appropriate sales tax.) For billed orders, cost per copy is $9.95 plus postage and handling. (Prices subject to change without notice.)

Bulk orders (ten or more copies) of any individual sourcebook are available at the following discounted prices: 10–49 copies, $8.95 each; 50–00 copies, $7.96 each; over 100 copies, *inquire.* Sales tax and postage and handling charges apply as for single copy orders.

To ensure correct and prompt delivery, all orders must give either the *name of an individual* or an *official purchase order number.* Please submit your order as follows:

> *Subscriptions:* specify series and year subscription is to begin.
> *Single Copies:* specify sourcebook code (such as, IR1) and first two words of title.

Mail orders for United States and Possessions, Latin America, Canada, Japan, Australia, and New Zealand to:
> Jossey-Bass Inc., Publishers
> 433 California Street
> San Francisco, California 94104

Mail orders for all other parts of the world to:
> Jossey-Bass Limited
> 28 Banner Street
> London EC1Y 8QE

New Directions for Institutional Research Series
Patrick T. Terenzini, *Editor-in-Chief*
Marvin W. Peterson, *Associate Editor*

IR1 *Evaluating Institutions for Accountability,* Howard R. Bowen
IR2 *Assessing Faculty Effort,* James I. Doi
IR3 *Toward Affirmative Action,* Lucy W. Sells
IR4 *Organizing Nontraditional Study,* Samuel Baskin
IR5 *Evaluating Statewide Boards,* Robert O. Berdahl
IR6 *Assuring Academic Progress Without Growth,* Allan M. Cartter

IR7   *Responding to Changing Human Resource Needs,* Raul Heist, Jonathan R. Warren

IR8   *Measuring and Increasing Academic Productivity,* Robert A. Wallhaus

IR9   *Assessing Computer-Based System Models,* Thomas R. Mason

IR10   *Examining Departmental Management,* James Smart, James Montgomery

IR11   *Allocating Resources Among Departments,* Paul L. Dressel, Lou Anna Kimsey Simon

IR12   *Benefiting from Interinstitutional Research,* Marvin W. Peterson

IR13   *Applying Analytic Methods to Planning and Management,* David S. P. Hopkins, Roger G. Scroeder

IR14   *Protecting Individual Rights to Privacy in Higher Education,* Alton L. Taylor

IR15   *Appraaising Information Needs of Decision Makers,* Carl R. Adams

IR16   *Increasing the Public Accountability of Higher Education,* John K. Folger

IR17   *Analyzing and Constructing Cost,* Meredith A. Gonyea

IR18   *Employing Part-Time Faculty,* David W. Leslie

IR19   *Using Goals in Research and Planning,* Robert Fenske

IR20   *Evaluating Faculty Performance and Vitality,* Wayne C. Kirschling

IR21   *Developing a Total Marketing Plan,* John A. Lucas

IR22   *Examining New Trends in Administrative Computing,* E. Michael Staman

IR23   *Professional Development for Institutional Research,* Robert G. Cope

IR24   *Planning Rational Retrenchment,* Alfred L. Cooke

IR25   *The Impact of Student Financial Aid on Institutions,* Joe B. Henry

IR26   *The Autonomy of Public Colleges,* Paul L. Dressel

IR27   *Academic Program Evaluation,* Eugene C. Craven

IR28   *Academic Planning for the 1980s,* Richard B. Heydinger

IR29   *Institutional Assessment for Self-Improvement,* Richard I. Miller

IR30   *Coping with Faculty Reduction,* Stephen R. Hample

IR31   *Evaluation of Management and Planning Systems,* Nick L. Poulton

IR32   *Increasing the Use of Program Evaluation,* Jack Lindquist

IR33   *Effective Planned Change Strategies,* G. Melvin Hipps

IR34   *Qualitative Methods for Institutional Research,* Eileen Kuhns, S. V. Martorana

IR35   *Information Technology: Advances and Applications,* Bernard Sheehan

IR36   *Studying Student Attrition,* Ernest T. Pascarella

IR37   *Using Research for Strategic Planning,* Norman P. Uhl

IR38   *The Politics and Pragmatics of Institutional Research,* James W. Firnberg, William F. Lasher

IR39   *Applying Methods and Techniques of Futures Research,* James L. Morrison, William L. Renfro, Wayne I. Boucher

IR40   *College Faculty: Versatile Human Resources in a Period of Constraint,* Roger G. Baldwin, Robert T. Blackburn

IR41   *Determining the Effectiveness of Campus Services,* Robert A. Scott

IR42   *Issues in Pricing Undergraduate Education,* Larry H. Litten

IR43   *Responding to New Realities in Funding,* Larry L. Leslie

IR44   *Using Microcomputers for Planning and Management Support,* William L. Tetlow

IR45   *Impact and Challenges of a Changing Federal Role,* Virginia Ann Hodgkinson

IR46   *Institutional Research in Transition,* Marvin W. Peterson, Mary Corcoran

Contents

Editor's Notes   1
Peter T. Ewell

Chapter 1. Perspectives and Problems in Student   7
Outcomes Research
C. Robert Pace
Many tests and techniques have been developed to measure the impact of
college on students. Which to use depends on the institution's educa-
tional goals and on the content of each student's educational experience.

Chapter 2. Use of Outcomes Information at the University of   19
Tennessee, Knoxville
Trudy W. Banta
For one large public research university, a statewide performance fund-
ing initiative provided a strong incentive to examine student outcomes.
The result has been a systematic program of data collection and dissem-
ination that has had a significant impact both on the curriculum and on
the university's budgeting process.

Chapter 3. Using Outcomes Assessment: A Case Study in   33
Institutional Change
Charles J. McClain, Darrell W. Krueger
At a critical point in one university's history, a value-added student
assessment model was developed. Data generated by the model have been
used to improve student learning and development throughout the curriculum, and they have helped the university to clarify and revitalize its
mission.

Chapter 4. Assessing and Validating the Outcomes of College   47
Marcia Mentkowski, Georgine Loacker
A multifaceted assessment process allows the development of each stu-
dent to be observed and improved as she moves through the curriculum.
A corresponding evaluating process allows the content of curricula to be
validated against external, real-world standards.

Chapter 5. Developing and Using a Longitudinal Student   65
Outcomes Data File: The University of Colorado Experience
Jean Endo, Terry Bittner
Constructing a longitudinal student outcomes data file takes careful
planning and attention to detail, but investment in such a resource
yields substantial dividends in the ability to document and explain complex patterns of student success.

**Chapter 6. Designing Follow-Up Studies of Graduates and
Former Students**   81
Mike Stevenson, R. Dan Walleri, Saundra M. Japely

The results of student outcomes studies are of little value if they are
not used in institutional planning and decision making. Use of results
can be made more effective if researchers understand the obstacles to
information use on most college campuses and tailor their presentations
to overcome them.

Chapter 7. Increasing the Use of Student Outcomes Information   93
Mary K. Kinnick

The results of student outcomes studies are of little value if they are
not used in institutional planning and decision making. Use of results
can be made more effective if researchers understand the obstacles to
information use on most college campuses and tailor their presentations
to overcome them.

Chapter 8. Some Implications for Practice   111
Peter T. Ewell

Successful outcomes assessment programs have many common
characteristics. Institutional researchers should seek to recognize these
signs of success and use them as guides for developing their own campus
programs.

Appendix   121
Peter T. Ewell

Some common sources of student outcomes information.

Index   125

For information about the Association for Institutional Research, write:

AIR Executive Office
314 Stone Building
Florida State University
Tallahassee, FL 32306

(904) 644-4470

Editor's Notes

Institutional researchers are often called on to implement or coordinate campus-based studies of student attitudes, student achievement, or student occupational and career development during or after college. Such studies—generally grouped under the heading of student outcome studies—are increasingly being mandated by state or system offices in the public sector of higher education, and they are increasingly being required or strongly suggested by regional or professional accreditation bodies. Such studies are also in demand at the institutional level, because they are useful in shaping the curriculum and in developing more effective strategies for student recruitment and retention. This volume has three purposes: to give institutional researchers an overview of the many facets of research on student outcomes, to show how outcomes research programs have been organized and implemented in various settings, and to provide some basic technical advice about the design of particular types of studies and the communication of results.

New Demand for Outcomes Assessment

Concern with assessment of student outcomes has risen sharply over the past decade, and many factors have been responsible. First, all levels of authority have become increasingly concerned about the allocation of limited educational resources for maximum effectiveness. As financial constraints have tightened, legislators and others responsible for providing public higher education with resources have become anxious to have evidence of the return on their investment. At the institutional level, college and university administrators must increasingly fund needed improvements by reallocating existing resources. Both concerns demand ways of assessing the degree to which educational objectives have been attained.

At the same time, concern about the quality of American postsecondary education has emerged. Following hard on a series of critical assessments of elementary and secondary education, similar questions are now being directed at our colleges and universities. Falling test scores, declines in general education, and high attrition rates have all been deemed symptomatic of an erosion of quality at the baccalaureate level (NIE Study Group, 1984).

As a result of these concerns, explicit institution-based studies of student learning and development are increasingly being required or encouraged by both public and private higher education agencies. For the past five years, the Tennessee Higher Education Commission (THEC) has operated a performance-funding program that uses specified outcomes criteria to allocate a portion of state higher education dollars to individual institutions. In Florida, all public university students must pass a common college-level academic skills test in order to attain junior standing. In South Dakota, public universities are requiring demonstrated performance on tests in the major field as a criterion for successful completion of a program. In Missouri, Mississippi, and several other states, graduates of baccalaureate programs in particular fields (notably teacher education) are now required to pass a common standardized examination as a condition of graduation. Many other examples could be cited; more are emerging every month.

While the efforts just outlined have been directed primarily at public institutions, private colleges and universities have also been affected by this trend. Several regional accreditation organizations have increased their attention to outcomes assessment in the institutional accreditation process. Most recently, the Southern Association of Colleges and Schools adopted an institutional effectiveness criterion that calls for the explicit assessment of student outcomes. Similar bodies, notably the North Central Association and Middle States Association of Colleges and Schools, have long encouraged institutions to conduct such assessments as part of the self-study process (Thrash, 1984). Finally, national panels, such as the NIE Study Group on the Conditions of Excellence in American Postsecondary Education, have strongly linked outcomes assessment with institutional improvement (NIE Study Group, 1984) and suggest that assessment be a major part of any institution's quest for quality.

More important than external mandates is the growing recognition among college and university administrators that assessment of student outcomes can yield considerable dividends. The results of such assessments can be used to improve retention and recruitment strategies, to identify problems within particular curricula, or to establish the need for increasing the emphasis on particular skills areas across the curriculum. They can be used to improve program articulation with primary feeder institutions on the one hand and with the institutions and professions that receive graduates on the other. They can be used to revise and evaluate particular service or support functions across the campus. Most important, they can help to focus institutional attention on its most critical activities, teaching and learning.

Institutional research offices are natural recipients of requests for studies of student outcomes. They are centrally located, they have access to significant arrays of data, and they have established a network for disseminating information throughout the institution. Few such offices currently conduct assessments of student outcomes on a regular basis. One reason is the nature of the field itself: Outcomes assessments can range in content from cognitive development in college to career achievement after graduation and in technical complexity from simple surveys of currently enrolled students to carefully designed longitudinal assessments employing sophisticated psychological measurement instruments. As Chapter One emphasizes, there are many assessment instruments and processes from which to choose. In order to make an informed choice, the researcher must be clear about which kinds of outcomes to look at and why.

What Are Student Outcomes?

There are about as many different typologies of student outcomes as there are individuals who have investigated the field. All the typologies make a number of distinctions in common. These distinctions help institutional researchers to make some basic choices about what to investigate and why. For example, the distinction between cognitive and affective outcomes is a distinction between gains in knowledge on the one hand and changes in attitudes or values on the other. Increased knowledge about American history or increased ability to reason analytically are examples of the former; changes in liberalism, tolerance, or acquisitiveness are examples of the latter. The distinction between psychological and behavioral outcomes is a distinction between changes occurring inside a student's head and changes that can be observed directly during or after college. Actual student mastery of the concepts of physics or ability to think critically are examples of the former; job performance after graduation or voluntary withdrawal from an institution or program are examples of the latter. Finally, the distinction between within-college and after-college outcomes is a distinction about when the outcome occurs. A student's decision to change majors or the learning experience in a particular curriculum are examples of the former; attainment of an advanced degree at another institution or a retrospective evaluation of the college environment long after graduation are examples of the latter.

Such distinctions as these combine and interact in many ways. At the same time, different clusters of distinctions define relatively distinct sets of research activities. For example, assessments of learning gain are generally cognitive, psychological, and within-college. Such assessments require careful instrumentation, and they often use before-and-after testing to determine value added. More familiar to institutional researchers are affective and behavioral studies based on student surveys, which can be administered both to currently enrolled students and to graduates or former students. Such studies employ methodologies quite different from those of learning gain studies and deal with such issues as sample selection, survey design, and assessment of questionnaire bias. Finally, many outcomes studies are purely behavioral and within-college, for example, studies of course-taking patterns, changes in student major and status, and retention studies based entirely on existing institutional records. All such inquiries have their place in a comprehensive outcomes assessment program. One purpose of this volume is to show how different kinds of outcomes studies can be designed and undertaken.

More important than individual study design is the way in which different kinds of studies can combine and interact in the context of a broad outcomes assessment program. An institution's assessment program depends on its mission and the problems it faces. Thus, the second purpose of the volume is to illustrate some of the basic choices that must be made in designing a comprehensive institutional outcomes assessment program.

Organization of This Volume

Given these major purposes, the volume is divided into three sections. The first section consists of a single chapter. In Chapter One, Bob Pace of U.C.L.A. reviews some milestones of student outcomes research in order to highlight some major issues involved in the conduct of outcomes studies. Pace emphasizes that student outcomes assessment is not new and illustrates some of the basic assessment techniques and instruments that can be used to investigate the impact of college on students. He also distinguishes among the many different types of outcomes studies and considers some broad issues of outcomes assessment that any practitioner is likely to encounter. These issues include objections to measurement of student development per se, student self-reports as evidence of learning gain, and determination of the proper unit of analysis for outcomes studies.

The second section shows how these issues develop in practice. Chapter Two, by Trudy Banta of the University of Tennessee, Knoxville, describes the experience of a large public research university under Tennessee's performance-funding program. Chapter Three, by Charles McClain and Darrell Krueger of Northeast Missouri State University, describes a value-added assessment program at a medium-sized public institution. Chapter Four, by Marcia Mentkowski and Georgine Loacker of Alverno College, describes a comprehensive program for the assessment of student development and the evaluation of learning gains in a small private liberal arts college. All three efforts have achieved national recognition and can justly serve as examples to others. However, each program is distinctive, and none should prompt direct imitation. Rather, the authors describe the choices made in designing each effort, which should prove instructive to anyone attempting to establish a similar program in an equally distinctive institutional environment.

The third section consists of three practice-oriented chapters on the methodology of student outcomes assessment. In Chapter Five, Jean Endo and Terry Bittner of the University of Colorado at Boulder cover the basic practical issues involved in using questionnaires and existing student records to design a longitudinal student outcomes data base. The authors address such issues as the identification and tracking of student cohorts, the integration of data from student data base records with questionnaire data, the timing of student surveys, and the reporting of results to campus administrators. In Chapter Six, Mike Stevenson, Dan Walleri, and Saundra

Japely of Mt. Hood Community College cover the major practical issues involved in surveying students after they have left the institution, either as graduates or as former students. The issues covered include identification of the study population, choice or design of the instrument, sampling and survey strategies, and use of the results of such studies. Finally, in Chapter Seven, Mary Kinnick of Portland State University presents some techniques for communicating the results of outcomes studies to different decision-making constituencies inside and outside the institution. One of the greatest obstacles that practicing institutional researchers face is the problem of presenting the results of outcomes studies so that they can be used effectively. This chapter discusses some techniques developed in the course of a national project on the effective utilization of student outcomes information.

The lessons of these seven chapters are many, and they are summarized in Chapter Eight. An appendix contains an annotated list of some of the most popular instruments for assessing the impact of college on students. Each instrument is briefly described, and information on how to obtain it is given.

The assessment of student outcomes is a large, complex, and currently much-debated topic—one that no single volume can expect to cover adequately. At the same time, it is a topic about which one learns by doing. The ultimate value of the cases presented here will be measured not by the number of citations that they generate but by the ideas that practicing researchers garner from them and by the campus-based research programs that these ideas are used to build or improve.

Peter T. Ewell
Editor

References

NIE Study Group on the Conditions of Excellence in American Higher Education. *Involvement in Learning: Realizing the Potential of American Higher Education.* Washington, D.C.: U.S. Government Printing Office, 1984.

Thrash, P. "Accreditation and the Evaluation of Educational Outcomes: A Regional Accreditor's Perspective." Paper presented at a professional development session sponsored by the Council of Specialized Accrediting Agencies and the Council on Postsecondary Accreditation, Chicago, April 1984.

Peter T. Ewell is a senior associate at the National Center for Higher Education Management Systems (NCHEMS). He directs the NCHEMS/Kellogg Student Outcomes Project. His major research interests are the impact of college on students and the organizational uses of data and information.

Over the years, many tests and techniques have been developed to measure the impact of college on students. Which to use depends on the institution's educational goals and on the content of each student's educational experience.

Perspectives and Problems in Student Outcomes Research

C. Robert Pace

Would anyone be better qualified to assess what young Alexander was learning than his tutor Aristotle? Surely, Aristotle's assessment would reflect an intimate knowledge of what he was trying to teach, and it would be based on direct, daily, personal observation of what his pupil was learning. Viewed from the perspective provided by this example, the assessment of student outcomes is probably as old as recorded history.

However, the example of Aristotle and Alexander may be of little comfort to the director of institutional research who has just been assigned the responsibility for developing a program to evaluate student outcomes at his or her college. The director's problem is more complicated. What does one substitute for Aristotle, who provides the informed judgments? What does one do when there are one or ten thousand Alexanders studying different subjects under different people and when each Alexander has different experiences that contribute to his learning and personal growth? In language of education, the questions are these: First, what are the goals or objectives of college education? Second, what evidence indicates that these goals have been attained? Third, how does one define outcomes— immediate, long-range, specific, general?

P. T. Ewell (Ed.). *Assessing Educational Outcomes.* New Directions for Institutional Research, no. 47. San Francisco: Jossey-Bass, September 1985.

Nationally Normed Achievement Tests

Almost everyone will agree on the importance of two student outcomes: the acquisition of knowledge and the development of intellectual skills. What do students learn? How well do they think? Thus, the first question is, What is available for judging students' progress or attainment in these respects?

A number of objective tests of school learning have been constructed in this century—tests of basic skills in reading comprehension and arithmetic, tests of knowledge of the subject matter commonly taught in elementary and secondary schools. Statewide testing programs are often mandatory. Age and grade norms are common. In higher education, well-constructed objective achievement tests both in broad fields of knowledge and in specific college subjects can be used in assessing student outcomes. When the Educational Testing Service (ETS) was founded in 1948, the Cooperative Test Service and the Graduate Record Examination (GRE) program had already developed standardized tests in general mathematics, physical science, biological science, history and social studies, literature, arts, effectiveness of expression, vocabulary, and current social problems. These tests became parts of the ETS inventory. New tests were developed, and they are available for use or reference today.

The Graduate Record Examination board has subject tests in seventeen fields—biology, chemistry, computer science, economics, education, engineering, French, geology, history, English literature, mathematics, music, physics, political science, psychology, sociology, and Spanish. These GRE tests are intended for college seniors; results are used mainly in screening students for admission to graduate school, but they need not be limited to that use. The Undergraduate Assessment Program at the ETS has area tests in humanities, science, and social science, which are pitched at a level that makes them suitable for undergraduates who do not plan to enter graduate school. These tests could be given to sophomores and seniors, and the differences could be noted.

The College Board and ETS have a variety of achievement tests in the College-Level Examination Program (CLEP). These tests are intended for persons who want to demonstrate mastery of college-level material and receive credit or course exemption for their knowledge. There are thirty course exams. The content of the exams reflects what is currently taught in college courses; the test makers periodically update the tests to reflect changes that have occurred in the course content. Regular students who have completed a course take the CLEP test so that the college can have a local baseline for the award of credit to persons who have not taken the course. These up-to-date achievement tests could be used on a very broad scale. In addition, the CLEP has general examinations of English composition, humanities, mathematics, natural sciences, social sciences, and history. These general exams can be used to assess the outcomes of general education.

Another nationally normed test that is now in wide use, the college admissions test of the American College Testing (ACT) program, could be used to assess students' learning during the first two years of college. The achievement tests in English, mathematics, science, and social science that compose it were designed to measure what students learn in high school. The tests could be repeated after students have spent a year or two in college to see whether their scores increase. The fact that the ACT instruments test achievement in common high school subjects that are similar to college subjects makes them appropriate for assessing growth after college entrance. One reservation must be noted: If a student scores very high on the test at the time of admission, the test will not reveal growth on readministration. It is most appropriately used with students whose entrance scores are close to the average or below average.

The newest set of achievement measures that has gained national recognition was produced by the College Outcomes Measures Project (COMP) at ACT. This test battery is oriented toward the application of facts, concepts, and skills believed to be relevant for three areas of adult life: functioning within social institutions, using science and technology, and using the arts. In each of these areas, the tests measure competence in communicating, solving problems, and clarifying social values. The stimulus materials resemble materials that one encounters in adult life: film excerpts, taped newscasts, advertisements, art prints, photographs, music, graphs, stories, and magazine articles. Students respond to these materials in writing or speech. The responses cannot be scored like answers to an objective achievement test, so trained judges must rate each student's response. The process is very time-consuming and very expensive. An objective version of the COMP test uses the same stimulus materials. Students respond by selecting from among options; two of the four are regarded as good answers. COMP materials have been used with adult groups as well as with college students. One caution is in order: The test content has little relationship to the content of the academic disciplines or the broad areas of knowledge taught in college. In one sense, this makes it unique, but in another sense it limits its value for measuring the outcomes of what colleges teach.

All the achievement tests produced by the GRE, the College Board, and the ETS measure basic intellectual skills as well as knowledge. For the most part, the test items ask students to interpret and understand knowledge by drawing appropriate generalizations from the material that is presented, by interpreting graphs and tables, by deducing, analyzing, extrapolating; these are all important intellectual skills. Likewise, the ACT admissions test battery measures students' ability to interpret reading materials in the field, not just to recall facts.

In the early 1950s, the Cooperative Study of Evaluation in General Education constructed a number of special tests to measure critical thinking. Dressel and Mayhew (1954) describe the instruments developed to test critical thinking in social science, reading and writing, science, and the humanities as well as a general test of critical thinking. At the conclusion of the study, these tests were filed with the ETS. The authors provide many examples of test items as well as extensive and explicit analyses of the objectives and the test blueprints.

There are other well-constructed achievement tests and tests of intellectual skills. I cannot hope to cite them all in this brief chapter. If one goal of a student outcomes evaluation program is to determine what students have learned about broad fields of knowledge and about various major fields of specialization, there are good instruments for that purpose, and there are many good models that one can use if one wants to construct instruments of one's own.

Measures of Interests, Values, and Personal Traits

Statements about the goals of college education almost always include aspects of personality and character as well as intellect. Development of these aspects is seldom an explicit teaching goal of courses in the academic disciplines, but all faculty members attach some importance to such traits as honesty, objectivity, tolerance, and self-understanding. Moreover, college is a social as well as an intellectual environment, a place where one meets new people, learns to deal with new challenges in human relationships, and confronts one's own values and ethical standards. We can hope that these experiences will be positive and rewarding, but for some students they may be traumatic and negative. In contrast to knowledge and intellectual skills, which cannot possibly decline under instruction, many attributes of personality and character can change in positive or negative directions. It is not an objective of higher education to undermine self-esteem or to retard the development of independence and ego strength; nor is it an objective of higher education to make students more liberal or more conservative politically, whatever that may mean today. Moreover, few personality tests have been built for the purpose of determining how the experience of college changes attitudes, interests, or values. Nevertheless, we should have some concern for what happens to people in these areas whether or not affective development is part of the curriculum.

There are more tests of personality characteristics than I can list or comment on here. The task of the institutional research director is to decide whether the information that a particular personality test provides is relevant to the assessment of student outcomes. My own opinion is that many personality tests are not appropriate for use in an evaluation of higher education, partly because what they measure is not clearly related to educational objectives, partly because some personality traits are rather deeply embedded by the time a student reaches college age, and spending a few years in college is unlikely to change them in any highly visible way.

Three tests merit at least some consideration: the Vocational Preference Inventory by Holland (1973), because so many students are concerned about the vocational relevance of their college education; the Terminal and Instrumental Values Scales by Rokeach (1969), because some shifts in the priority of values may be attributable to the influence of college; and the Omnibus Personality Inventory by Heist and Yonge (1962), because some of its subscores are relevant to educational purposes, especially the scales that define a variable called Intellectual Disposition.

Judgments of Expert Observers

I claimed at the outset of this chapter that Aristotle was a well-qualified judge of Alexander's learning because he had frequent, perhaps even daily, opportunities to observe his pupil directly. Is this not true of many faculty members today? Surely no one is better qualified to say what a student knows about chemistry than the man or woman who teaches the chemistry course. The difficulty in using faculty for the assessment of student outcomes lies in the fact that different professors have different criteria for judging students' performance. To the extent that teachers assign grades on some sort of curve, the grades have no meaning beyond the particular students who take the course at any one time. However, if the college and the professors have some basic criteria for good performance, then the professors' grades may have some relevance as assessments of outcomes. When there are accepted criteria for performance, it becomes possible to observe how many students attain the desired level.

The outcomes that cannot be attributed to the subject matter of courses are likely to be related to experiences outside class, interpersonal associations, involvement in clubs and organizations, residence hall activities, and so forth. In these cases, the expert judges are those who have the best opportunity to observe behavior in nonacademic situations: counselors, residence hall advisers, sponsors of student clubs and extracurricular projects. The problems for assessment here are the availability of qualified judges and the consistency of their judgments.

Local Assessments

Every college, curriculum, and student body is in some respects unique. In higher education, there are no identical twins. Standardized achievement tests and tests of basic personality characteristics measure what is standard, common, or typical, not what is unique. Of course, there is a great deal of similarity among programs of higher education. The subject matter of a basic chemistry course surely has some elements in common with similar courses on other campuses. Most curricula consist of courses that can be readily classified as sciences, humanities, or social sciences. But, because each college has its own students, courses, requirements, and faculty, each college may wish to devise its own program for assessing student outcomes. While it is important for a college to know how its student outcomes compare with student outcomes at other colleges, it is also important for the college to know whether some special local emphasis produces a special outcome.

Classic examples come from Syracuse, the General College at Minnesota, Antioch, Pennsylvania College for Women, San Francisco State, Stephens, Chicago City Junior College, the University of Florida, Western Washington College of Education, the School of Science at Purdue, Drake, Michigan State, and Chicago. Most of these assessments employ a mix of locally devised measures and published tests. They developed questionnaires to measure attitudes and satisfaction. They sought evidence of personal and social development as well as of cognitive development, and faculty and administrators were interested in and committed to the process and results of evaluation efforts. Most of the reports also reveal that evaluation, learning, and instruction are very similar activities. They involve clarifying what one intends to do, planning how to do it, carrying out the activities aimed at accomplishing the goals, and judging how well one has done. Moreover, since the concern is with outcomes of programs, all those who devise and carry out programs have a potential interest in participating in the process of evaluation.

It is possible for some third party to conduct a student outcomes assessment, but the result of such detached activitiy may have little influence on the college. If learning is the purpose of evaluation, then the participants in evaluation activities should be regarded as learners. This does not mean that they must devise all the evaluation instruments, but it does mean that they must help to select the instruments and that they must agree that the instruments will provide answers to questions they regard as important; it also means that they must participate in interpreting the results and in discussing and deciding how the program can be modified to produce better results.

Students as Reporters and Judges

We sometimes forget that nearly all the evidence we have about student outcomes comes from students themselves—from their answers to achievement test items, personality test items, and questionnaires that we devise. Relatively little evidence comes from other sources: faculty members, counselors, or student personnel staff.

We interpret students' responses to achievement or personality tests.

However, students themselves are the interpreters of another kind of student response. How much do they think they have learned or gained in knowledge, intellectual skills, and personal and social development? What do they think about the college's programs and services? What activities have they engaged in during college? How well-prepared do they think they are for further education or for employment?

Too often we are inclined to dismiss their opinions as invalid or biased. This is a mistake. All the evidence that we have indicates that college students are conscientious and generally accurate reporters about their activities, that they express their opinions and satisfactions forthrightly, and that their judgments of what they have gained are consistent both with external evidence, when it exists, and with what we might expect in the light of their activities and interest. Much of this evidence has been reported by Pace (1984). So, we should look carefully at this source of evidence about student outcomes. Even if there is some discrepancy between the evidence from different sources, the fact remains that what students perceive to be true or characteristic is a reality in its own right, a condition that has its own inherent validity.

The ACT Evaluation Survey Service (1981) is a comprehensive and relevant set of questionnaires about student opinons and their estimates of progress. There are nine survey instruments in the set. Several are especially relevant for outcomes assessment at four-year colleges: an entering student survey, a student opinion survey intended for current students from end-of-year freshmen to end-of-year seniors, a withdrawing/nonreturning student survey, and an alumni survey. In addition to these basic questionnaires for the traditional college student, there are questionnaires for two-year colleges, adults, and high school students who have not yet entered college. The total package is comprehensive. Moreover, every questionnaire allows a college to add as many as thirty questions of its own choice. The results are reported back to the college. Results can include many subgroup results as well as totals for the population and normative or composite data for all users of the questionnaire. These questionnaires could be used to design a longitudinal study: That is, the same cohort could be administered the entering student survey, then the current student survey, then either the withdrawing student survey or the alumni survey. The fact that additional questions can be asked on each survey means that any college can use these instruments and still meet its own special purpose.

The college student experiences questionnaire by Pace (1983) offers a unique perspective and insight on student outcomes assessment. It asks students to indicate how much gain or progress they feel they have made with respect to twenty-one objectives. Its unique feature is a set of scales measuring the quality of effort that students put into using the facilities and opportunities that college provides for their learning and growth— basic facilities, such as classroom, library, laboratory, dormitory, student union, cultural facilities, recreational facilities, and opportunities for association and growth, such as clubs and organizations, contacts with faculty, student acquaintances, and writing experiences. Each scale consists of a list of activities that range from moderate to major potential for influencing learning and development; students indicate about how often during the current school year they have engaged in each activity. With respect to the library, for example, the activity "ran down leads, looked for further references that were cited in things you read" is a major use of the library's potential, whereas the activity "used the library as a quiet place to read or study material you brought with you" makes little use of what a library is all about. In addition to providing a systematic, theory-based, pragmatic inventory of what students do and of the progress that they believe they have made, the questionnaire collects some background information about the students, assesses their satisfaction with college, and asks them to characterize various aspects of the college environment. Results from this instrument show that students' quality of effort is the best predictor of attainment and that the breadth or scope of high-quality student effort may be an excellent indicator of the quality of undergraduate education on a campus.

Alumni as Reporters

Surveys of alumni provide further evidence of outcomes. Alumni are educational products in the years after graduation, just as students are educational products during the college years. The aims of education are typically expressed as desired changes: The individual is to know more, think more clearly, write more effectively, develop a greater appreciation of literature and the arts, acquire a better understanding of self, others, social institutions, or history, and so on. These are the sorts of changes that one seeks to observe during college. What behavior can one observe five, ten, or even twenty years after college that might be interpreted as outcomes of college? Is the question even appropriate?

The most conspicuous difference between college graduates and others lies in their occupations. Graduates comprise 100 percent or nearly so of people in the upper echelons of business, industry, finance, and government; in medicine, law, education, science and technology; and in many other fields. Typically, these fields require or expect education beyond college in graduate and professional school. If one is interested in the occupational relevance of college, one must wait until graduate or professional school training has been completed, for it is there that an increasing number of students become prepared for their work beyond college.

Most alumni surveys have consequently focused on occupational and economic status, success in further education, retrospective opinions about the benefits of college, and satisfaction with the college experience.

During college the direction of our inquiry is from college to the individual. What does college contribute to the student's learning and development? Beyond college, in the larger society, the direction can be reversed. What does the individual contribute to society? What do college graduates contribute to the welfare of the communities in which they live? Do they take part in the political processes that influence the quality of government? Do they contribute to the cultural enrichment of society by supporting libraries, art galleries, concerts, and theater? Do they exhibit in their personal lives the dimensions of character that one might expect of educated adults? And, since college is part of the larger society, what use do they make of it, and what do they do to maintain the quality of educational institutions? One could construct an alumni survey questionnaire around these and other topics. Pace (1983) provides examples of alumni surveys that have a broad scope of content.

Current and Persistent Problems

Alumni surveys are a good example of a general problem in all assessment research: How much time can elapse between an educational event and measurement of its outcome? This problem is interwoven with another: Is the event very specific and of short duration, or is it general in scope and extended over a period of time? A one-term course in English literature is a specific, short-term event. The reading that one does during four years of college is a general, lengthy event. A student's score on the final exam in an English literature course can be attributed to the student's having taken the course. If one were skeptical about the interpretation, one could give the test to people who were similar to the student in other respects but who did not take the course. To assess knowledge of literature as an outcome of four years of college, one can compare students' status at the beginning and the end of college, note the extent of reading done by students in different major fields, and determine whether those who read the most also gained the most. One could do this even without an objective measure of initial status simply by comparing self-reported progress with self-reported experience. With respect to alumni, one might want to predict that those who read more in college would twenty years later be reading more, buying more books, and patronizing the library more. So, is this an outcome of college? To expect the opposite, namely that students who read the most in college would read the least in later life, is surely unreasonable. Outcomes of college, for the most part, reveal continuity in individuals' lives. For nearly every individual, the aim of college is not to deny or reverse one's past but rather to build on it, to strengthen it, and to expand one's knowledge and one's personal and social development.

The notion of continuity is an important consideration when we compare longitudinal and cross sectional studies of outcomes. Many argue that only longitudinal studies are persuasive and valid for assessing outcomes. This is not true. There are periods in life history when change and development are dramatic, as in the first five years of life. Longitudinal studies are especially important in these periods. In other periods, for example, between the years of thirty and fifty, longitudinal data have relatively little importance. That the college years—age eighteen to twenty-two—require longitudinal data to assess outcomes is debatable.

It is true, of course, that educational objectives are typically stated as desired changes in students. That they are suggests the need for before-and-after measurement. Pretests and posttests are useful, but they are not always appropriate. Consider an absurd example. Suppose the aim of an instructional program in skiing is to enable a student to reach the bottom of an intermediate slope. Would it make any sense as a pretest to push the student down an intermediate slope to see how far he or she could go without falling or breaking a leg? Giving the final exam to students on the first day of a course would be of little use if the content of the course was highly specific and if it was very unlikely that the student would have encountered it elsewhere, but it may be very useful when the content is general and not esoteric. Pre- and posttesting pose another problem: The same test question does not always measure the same thing on the two tests. On the pretest, it may measure some aspect of critical thinking, but on the posttest, it may only be measuring recall of the method that the student used to solve the problem. Longitudinal studies can have yet another weakness: If they lose too many cases with the passage of time, the conclusions are based on what may be a very small and unrepresentative group of people. In some longitudinal studies spanning the four years of college, the group on which one has complete data is only 10 or 15 percent of the universe with which one began. Because of these weaknesses, it can be difficult to interpret single difference scores from before-and-after testing. These observations are not meant to suggest that longitudinal studies are not worth making; they are meant to suggest that longitudinal studies are not always more useful than cross sectional comparisons.

Concluding Observations

There are well-constructed tests of knowledge, intellectual skills, attitudes, interests, values, and personal traits. If they fit your objectives reasonably well, you should use them. They are reliable, and you can use the results to make comparisons with other students at other colleges. If you need to make your own tests, look at the test questions, rating scales, and opinion items that others have devised and used. Dressel and Mayhew (1954) are especially useful in this regard. The construction of a good questionnaire is not a simple task. One needs to be especially thoughtful about the wording of questions and about the context in which they are asked. Relatively small changes in the language can produce relatively large changes in the answers. Confidence in the meaning of answers does not depend on the size of the sample; it depends on the relevance, clarity, and quality of the question.

Use expert judges when you can. Expert judges can be defined as people who have both the best opportunity to observe and the appropriate standards of judgment. Remember that students may be the only qualified reporters of their own activities and the only qualified judges about some kinds of outcomes. Surely, Alexander could report with some accuracy what he was learning from Aristotle.

When you interpret student outcomes, be sure you can answer the question, Outcomes of what? For example, if you give a general education achievement test to end-of-year sophomores and again to end-of-year seniors and if most students complete all or most of their general education course requirements during the first two years of college, the difference between sophomore and senior scores should probably be interpreted as evidence of memory or retention of knowledge. Use before-and-after measures when they are appropriate. Be sure the measures that you use are capable of revealing gains. It is interesting and useful to observe gains, although it is often very difficult to do so. However, outcomes can ultimately be defined as where one is now.

Take the point of view that the purpose of outcomes assessment is learning. What do you want to learn? How will you learn it? And, what will you do after you have learned it? Presumably, the learning will enrich understanding and inform judgments about the strengths and weaknesses of one's programs so that one can improve them. Participation in the learning may be an essential condition for subsequent action on what has been learned.

Design a program of outcomes assessment as a continuing, ongoing enterprise. This does not mean that every aspect of every program should be evaluated all the time. It is not feasible in a large, complex university. The focus can shift from year to year, so that many sorts of outcomes can be covered over a reasonable period of time. The design and the procedures are similar; only the specific content and the participants change. There may be a few centrally important outcomes that one may wish to assess annually so as to plot trends. It is probably more feasible to consider an evaluation cycle, perhaps lasting five years, that corresponds to student generations or to major changes in college programs.

Last, do not expect minor changes in programs to produce major changes in outcomes. If you choose to think big about the scope and significance of outcomes, then you must also think big about the magnitude of college experiences when you seek explanations for outcomes. There are many outcomes for which no precise explanations can be identified, and, as the importance of a given outcome increases, the likelihood that there will be a specific explanation for it decreases. Nevertheless, it is still an outcome, and its importance for educational evaluation in no way depends on one's ability to explain precisely why it occurs. The chapters that follow will illustrate the points just made here.

References

Dressel, P. (Ed.). *Evaluation in General Education*. Dubuque, Iowa: William C. Brown, 1954.

Dressel, P., and Mayhew, L. *General Education: Explorations in Evaluation*. Washington, D.C.: American Council on Education, 1954.

Heist, P., and Yonge, G. *Omnibus Personality Inventory*. New York: Psychological Corporation, 1962.

Holland, J. *Making Vocational Choices: A Theory of Careers*. Englewood Cliffs, N.J.: Prentice-Hall, 1973.

Pace, C. R. *Measuring Outcomes of College*. San Francisco: Jossey-Bass, 1979.

Pace, C. R. *College Student Experiences: A Questionnaire*. (2nd ed.) Los Angeles: U.C.L.A. Higher Education Research Institute, 1983.

Pace, C. R. *Measuring the Quality of College Student Experiences*. Los Angeles: U.C.L.A. Higher Education Research Institute, 1984.

Rokeach, M. *The Measurement of Values and Value System*. East Lansing: Michigan State University, 1969.

C. Robert Pace is professor of higher education and director of the Laboratory for Research on Higher Education at the University of California, Los Angeles. He is the author of many books on student learning and development, and his research on this topic spans a period of more than forty years.

For one large public research university, a statewide performance funding initiative provided a strong incentive to examine student outcomes. The result has been a systematic program of data collection and dissemination that has had a significant impact both on the curriculum and on the university's budgeting process.

Use of Outcomes Information at the University of Tennessee, Knoxville

Trudy W. Banta

In 1979, the Tennessee Higher Education Commission (THEC) created a powerful incentive for the state's public institutions of higher education to become involved in the assessment of educational outcomes. Tennessee became the first state to apply a set of academic performance criteria in funding state colleges and universities. This alternative to the traditional enrollment-driven formula was originally conceived of as an annual supplement that could be as much as 2 percent of the instructional component of each institution's education and general budget. In 1981, the performance standards were elaborated in such a way as to affect virtually every academic program, and in 1983, the potential value of the award was increased to 5 percent of the budget for instruction.

Eligibility for the performance-funding supplement is based on an institution's ability to demonstrate the quality of its academic programs in an annual report. There are five standards of quality (Tennessee Higher Education Commission, 1983): the percentage of programs eligible for accreditation that are accredited; the percentage of programs that have undergone peer review, that have administered a comprehensive exam to majors within a five-year period, or both (maximum credit is obtained if

P. T. Ewell (Ed.). *Assessing Educational Outcomes.* New Directions for Institutional Research, no. 47. San Francisco: Jossey-Bass, September 1985.

student performance on the field exam improves over time or if it exceeds that of students in similar programs at comparable institutions); value added by the general education component of the curriculum, as measured by the American College Testing (ACT) College Outcome Measures Project (COMP) exam (maximum credit is obtained if the mean score gain between freshman and senior years exceeds that calculated for a group of comparable institutions); opinion concerning the quality of academic programs and services, as measured by surveys of students, alumni, employers, or community members; and implementation of a campuswide plan for instructional improvement based on findings derived from the procedures just described as well as from other sources.

Due principally to the financial incentive offered by the THEC, the University of Tennessee, Knoxville (UTK) has developed a student outcomes assessment program that is comprehensive in scope: It attempts to furnish mutually supportive combinations of information and to explicitly encourage use of this information in improving academic programs and services throughout the institution. As a result of the adoption of appropriate new policies and procedures, student outcomes information has been woven into the fabric of planning and decision making at the institution.

Design of the Assessment

In 1981, central administrators at UTK undertook a formal study of the recently elaborated THEC performance-funding standards. The aim was to assess the potential impact of implementing the instructional evaluation program suggested by the standards on this campus of 26,000 students (20,000 undergraduates, 6,000 graduate students). In January 1982, a small grant for the study was obtained from the Kellogg Foundation through the National Center for Higher Education Management Systems (NCHEMS).

The student outcomes chosen for study at UTK were the outcomes emphasized in the THEC instructional evaluation schedule: achievement in general education, achievement in the major field, and opinion concerning the quality of academic programs and services (Tennessee Higher Education Commission, 1983). As the first step, the deans of the nine undergraduate colleges (agriculture, architecture, business, communications, education, engineering, home economics, liberal arts, and nursing) were interviewed to learn what kind of outcomes information was available in their college and how it was being used. The deans painted a rather bleak picture: Most had access to student evaluations of instruction and to some unit surveys of graduates. A few had files of student scores on licensing exams. Most reported that little or no use had been made of the information thus accumulated.

For each of the three outcomes areas, a task force composed of associate deans and faculty with appropriate expertise was formed to review the THEC guidelines and determine whether and how the specified standards could be addressed at UTK. The three task forces worked for a period of four months, then met as one group to review and consolidate recommendations.

Achievement in General Education. The general education task force included several members of the university's coordinating committee on general education. Shortly before, this committee had completed a campuswide study that defined general education competencies in terms of basic skills, knowledge, and judgment and attitudes. Its report was quite useful in the review of existing measures, because it provided a basis for assessing content validity. Only two sets of instruments were given serious consideration: the ACT COMP exam and activity inventory (Forrest, 1982) and a series of measures developed by McBer and Company (Winter and others, 1981). Task force members were quite interested in the McBer instruments but finally decided that their individualized nature made them impractical for administration to a representative sample of UTK students.

The task force selected the objective version of the ACT COMP test and recommended that it be administered annually to entering freshmen and graduating seniors. The six scales of the COMP test—Using Science, Using the Arts, Functioning in Social Institutions, Communicating, Solving Problems, and Clarifying Values—were found to contain items that would measure approximately half of the competencies described in the document prepared by the UTK coordinating committee on general education. The task force recommended that the COMP exam be supplemented with other measures as soon as better instruments were developed and the university could afford to administer them.

To ensure that representative samples of students would take the COMP exam, the faculty senate was asked to pass a testing requirement. A simple statement was adopted specifying that every student would participate prior to graduation in "one or more evaluative activities" designed to assist the university in assessing the quality of its academic programs.

Since the task force on general education made its recommendations in June 1982, the COMP exam has been administered to a systematic sample of freshmen during registration week of the fall quarter each year and to systematic samples of seniors during fall and spring quarters. The student samples are designed to be representative of the nine undergraduate colleges and of the distribution of student ability as indicated by the entering ACT composite score.

Achievement in the Major Field. Task force members investigating indicators of achievement in the major field believed that the THEC instructional evaluation standards placed too much emphasis on test scores. They advanced several reasons for this belief. First, the idea of using scores on a nationally standardized test, such as the Graduate Record Exam, or on a licensing exam, such as the Engineer-in-Training exam, to evaluate programs was somewhat new. The exam scores had been available for years, but faculty had viewed them as measures of individual student achievement, not as indicators of program strengths and weaknesses. In architecture, engineering, law, and social work, there was good reason for faculties not to consider the national exams as sources of program evaluation data: The only information provided by the organizations responsible for testing was the percentage of students who passed the test. The absence of subscores made it impossible to determine how a program could be improved. Finally, many faculty felt that national exams did not include the concepts they considered important in their teaching.

Measurement of achievement in the major field is ultimately the responsibility of individual faculties. Despite the problems involved, UTK faculties in nursing, education, engineering, architecture, business, and selected areas of liberal arts, such as physics, sociology, and German, have elected to use standardized exams to furnish evidence of program strengths and weaknesses. However, in some forty disciplines, no national exam is available, and faculties with little or no training in psychometrics must develop their own comprehensive exams. Nevertheless, two departments undertook pilot projects focused on test development in 1983, and faculty from these units have shared their experience with others.

In view of the shortcomings of test scores, the task force on achievement in the major field recommended that faculties supplement evaluative data from this source with information from one or more other sources: evaluation of comprehensive student achievement by faculty, external reviewers or both; end-of-program assessment by seniors reporting perceptions of their own achievement; retrospective assessment by alumni of their own achievement; and assessment by employers of the competencies of alumni one or more years after graduation.

Opinion Measures. The task force that considered the measurement of opinion about the quality of academic programs and services reviewed five instruments: the ACT student Opinion Survey, which had been administered twice at UTK in recent years; the NCHEMS/College Board Student Outcomes Information Service Surveys; the College Student Experiences Questionnaire by Robert Pace; the student information form offered by the Cooperative Institutional Research Program; and a survey developed at UTK that had been used in the past. The review convinced task force members that no existing instrument provided sufficient detail about the reasons for satisfaction or dissatisfaction with programs and services. Thus, the group recommended that one or more survey instruments be developed specifically for use on the Knoxville campus.

Two opinionnaires, the Student Satisfaction Survey (SSS) for enrolled students and the Survey of Graduates for alumni, were designed by faculty members in sociology and political science. Students, faculty, department heads, and student affairs directors were involved in the design of the SSS so that they would have a vested interest in the results obtained. The survey of graduates was developed in cooperation with the Planning and Budgeting Coordinating Committee for use by that group in environmental scanning.

The SSS was administered for the first time during the 1983 spring quarter. The survey was mailed to a sample of 2,200 enrolled undergraduates stratified by college and class (freshman, sophomore, junior, senior), and more than 70 percent returned it. The survey of graduates was mailed to more than 4,400 alumni in June 1984, and 69 percent of those sampled returned the instrument.

Culminating Activities. When the three task forces met in June 1982 to share findings, they reached a consensus on the need for promoting several campuswide initiatives. These initiatives included pilot projects in colleges and schools and the use of outcomes assessment information of several kinds in the university's comprehensive program review process. Going one step further, task force chancellor's staff and the Planning and Budgeting Coordinating Committee pay more attention to the program reviews when making strategic decisions about program mix and resource allocations.

The deans of the nine undergraduate colleges were asked to solicit proposals from departmental faculties for using one or more outcome measures to evaluate their programs. In January 1983, fourteen units in nine colleges received minigrants ranging from $350 to $1,500 to test methods of collecting and using student outcome information. Seven units proposed to select or design and then to administer a comprehensive exam for program majors. Seven other units chose to survey enrolled students, alumni, or employers in order to acquire evaluation data.

A new section on outcomes information was prepared for the self-study guidelines given to units preparing for comprehensive program reviews. Beginning in fall 1983, faculties were asked to include in the self-study document such evidence of program outcomes as students' comprehensive exam scores, student and alumni opinion concerning program quality, and data on placement of graduates. In fall 1984, the Planning and Budgeting Coordinating Committee began to use the expanded program reviews in determining which programs to strengthen with institutional resources, to maintain at current status, or to curtail.

Dissemination of Assessment Results

Results of the opinion surveys and achievement testing were summarized in several different formats to meet the needs of various audiences. For each assessment component, the chancellor of the university and his staff received a brief summary illustrated with tables as well as the full report. A separate presentation of the campuswide data was provided for the Planning and Budgeting Coordinating Committee, whose members include two vice-chancellors, two vice-provosts, several academic deans, and the current and past presidents of the faculty senate. The vice-chancellor for student affairs and his staff received detailed information derived from student responses to SSS questions concerning universitywide services, such as registration and the student counseling center. The provost provided time for the board of deans to receive a full report on the assessment of campus services as well as of academic programs.

The chief dissemination effort was aimed at department heads and faculty—the individuals most responsible for the quality of instruction and most capable of effecting improvements in academic programs. Each college received a report approximately fifteen pages in length summarizing the findings of the student outcomes information collected by and for the college during the previous year. A sample of the overall summary sheet for one college is displayed in Figure 1. College data derived from the COMP exam, tests in the major field, the student satisfaction survey, and the unit's own instruments were included. In 1984, alumni survey data were added. The pluses and minuses denote college means that were significantly above or below the universitywide averages.

Meetings were scheduled with faculty groups in each undergraduate college to present the student outcomes data summaries. In some cases, the report was presented at a general meeting of the entire college faculty. In other colleges, it was presented at a special meeting of an undergraduate curriculum committee or a committee charged with responsibility for improving teaching and learning. In all cases, the dean or the associate dean for undergraduate studies was present at the meeting with faculty. Most of the uses of outcomes information described later in this chapter can be attributed to the personal presentation of college-specific information to decision makers from that unit.

Leadership Structure

Leadership for the instructional evaluation program at UTK was provided by faculty associated with the Learning Research Center, an independent unit reporting directly to the provost. It has a universitywide mission to improve teaching and learning. The involvement of faculty in every aspect of the undertaking has given it credibility that is essential in convincing deans, department heads, and teaching faculty to use assessment results.

Perhaps the greatest strength of the assessment program at UTK lies in the extent to which it has involved virtually every major unit of the university and personnel at every level, ranging from students to the chancellor. Measurement activities in each of the three outcomes areas are carried

Figure 1. Sources of Instructional Evaluation Information for College D

Note: (+) or (−) Based on University Average; (0) = Lowest rating of all Colleges

I. Student Achievement
General Education
  Mean Entering ACT Score (+)
  Mean Total COMP Score (+)
  Estimated Gain on COMP (−)
Achievement in Major
  National Professional Exam

II. Other Sources
Dean's Follow-Up Survey of
  Seniors (Winter 1984)
Student Evaluations of
  Instruction

III. Student Ratings

Quality of Program Services in the Major—Table 12

Availability of Advisor	(0)
Willingness of Advisor to Help	(−)
Quality of Printed Program Information	(−)
Helpfulness of the Office Staff	(0)
Quality of Special Events	(−)
Adequacy of Preparation by Lower Division Courses for Upper Division Courses	(0)
Quality of Courses: Providing General Education	(−)
Quality of Courses: Preparing for Employment	(0)
Availability of Required Courses for the Major	(−)
Availability of Desired Courses for the Major	(−)
Organization of the Curriculum	(−)
Fairness of Grading	(−)
Quality of Instruction in Lower Division Courses in the Major	(0)
Quality of Instruction in Upper Division Courses in the Major	(−)
Opportunities for Interaction with Faculty in the Major	(0)
Practicum/Intern in the Major	(+)
Library Collection Related to the Major	(−)

Quality of Classroom Experience—Table 15

Comprehensiveness of Course Content	(−)
Relevance of Content for Student Needs	(0)
Extent to which Content is Current	(−)
Instructor's Class Presentations	(0)
Instructor's Class Preparation	(−)
Instructor's Enthusiasm for Teaching this Class	(−)
Instructor's Help with Problems	(−)
Fairness: Testing	(0)
Fairness: Grading	(−)
Clarity of Course Objectives	(−)
Conduciveness of Climate: Learning	(0)
Relevance of Lecture Information to Course Objectives	(0)
Quality of Classroom Discussion	(−)
Accuracy of Catalog Description: Course	(0)
Instructor's Knowledge of Subject Matter	(−)
Instructor's Availability for Consultation	(0)
Overall Quality of Instructor	(−)
Overall Quality of Course	(−)

Satisfaction with Social Experience at UTK	(+)
Satisfaction with Academic Experience at UTK	(+)

out independently, but the results are synthesized, interpreted, and disseminated by faculty in the Learning Research Center.

The film, slide, and audiocassette stimulus materials of the COMP exam are administered by experienced paraprofessionals under the supervision of a psychometrician from the Student Counseling Center (Division of Student Affairs) with assistance from the Educational Media Center (College of Education). The sample of seniors for the COMP exam is drawn by programmers in the Office of Student Data Analysis (Division of Student Affairs); the sample of entering freshmen is developed in the Office of Information Management Systems (Division of Business, Planning, and Finance). Students' achievement test scores are used first in the Records Office (Student Affairs) to determine which seniors have fulfilled the evaluation requirement prior to graduation; then they are stored permanently by the Office of Institutional Research (Business, Planning, and Finance). Survey data are stored at the campus Computing Center, an academic unit.

Uses of Assessment Information

The principal use of outcomes information at UTK has been to qualify for performance funding. With annual increases in the budget for higher education in Tennessee, the amounts for which UTK has been eligible have risen from $1.2 million in 1982 to $2.9 million in 1983 and $3.5 million in 1984. Learning Research Center personnel have compiled annual reports establishing the institution's eligibility for these funds. The greater challenge has been to involve central administrators, deans, directors, department heads, faculty, staff, and students in using the outcomes information to improve programs and services.

General Education. Change in general education is difficult to accomplish, since every faculty member is considered to play a role in providing this component of the curriculum, yet no unit is charged with administrative responsibility for it. Moreover, UTK COMP exam scores do not suggest the need for major changes, since the curriculum exhibits no specific weaknesses: The pattern of subscores is relatively flat year after year, the pattern of subscores for freshmen contains minor peaks and valleys in the same areas as the pattern for seniors does, and ACT reports that the score gain from freshman to senior year for UTK exceeds the mean calculated for a group of peer institutions. Nevertheless, the percentile rankings on all scales are lower than UTK faculty would like them to be, and this fact has stimulated interest in further analysis of the data and in certain faculty development activities.

Approximately twenty-five questions have been aded to the COMP exam to obtain information that may be related to achievement in general education. These items yield data on parents' level of education, patterns of course work in general education, and time spent studying, working, or participating in a variety of extracurricular activities. Two psychology professors are engaged in analyses that will identify relationships between these factors and gain on the COMP exam. Preliminary findings suggest that participation in student professional organizations is related to high achievement in general education. Several departments have used this information to encourage students to join existing organizations or to stimulate interest in starting new groups.

The structure of the COMP exam, which assesses students' ability to apply knowledge and to function effectively in adult roles, has implications for individual instructors. Aubrey Forrest, Director of the College Outcome Measures Project at ACT, has visited UTK twice to offer faculty development workshops on the content and structure of the exams.

Testing in the Major. During the past two years, forty academic programs at UTK have used a national standardized exam for majors to provide information that can be used for program evaluation. Two programs have developed their own exams, twenty are in the process of doing so, and twenty more are planning to develop exams in the next two years. To date, the programs that have invested time and effort in designing their own exams have made the most use of students' scores. These faculties have been more ego-involved in the outcomes of testing, since they made the decision about what content should be tested and by what means.

Faculties, such as those in psychology and microbiology, that selected national exams like the GRE advanced tests and then observed that their students scored well above the national averages understandably viewed the results as an endorsement of current practice and initiated no change. In contrast, the Department of English looked on somewhat lower scores on the GRE Advanced Test in Literature as confirming evidence of the need to tighten requirements for majors to ensure breadth of experience with literary classics. Seniors' scores on the Business Assessment Test (part of the ETS Undergraduate Assessment Program) convinced the business faculty to reduce the economics requirement so that a course in business law could be added to the curriculum.

The examination developed by faculty in the Department of Geography had sections on physical georgrapy, economic geography, cultural geography, and technique. Seniors attained high scores on the cultural section; their lowest scores were in economic geography. In view of the overall scores and the pattern of subscores, the faculty undertook several curriculum changes: Cultural geography was refocused, a course in economic geography was added to requirements for the major, and advisers began to encourage students to take a common core of courses. The department head said that in his judgment the greatest benefit of becoming involved in the test development project was that faculty members had been forced to consider the curriculum from the standpoint of measurement of outcomes—or the quality of the student product—not just in terms of general objectives that often reflected compromises among divergent views.

Faculty in the Department of Food Technology and Science in the College of Agriculture also developed their own test for seniors. That examination included sections on microbiology, food chemistry, meats, dairy products, and crop products. Faculty were not satisfied with seniors' scores on the microbiology and food chemistry sections. Students were not able to use their knowledge to solve problems as well as faculty had hoped they would be. After a series of meetings, the faculty who taught the courses in microbiology and food chemistry agreed to place additional emphasis on applications in their teaching and classroom tests. The food technology department head said that the experience of constructing the comprehensive exam had increased faculty competence as developers of classroom tests.

Opinion Surveys. Largely because the student satisfaction survey was developed by two UTK faculty members with recognized expertise in survey research and because these professors had involved administrators and faculty in reviewing drafts of their instrument, results of the surveys of enrolled students conducted in 1983 and 1984 have produced a number of significant changes, both at the campus and at the unit level.

Continuing evidence of student concern about the registration process and availability of courses prompted the vice-chancellor for student affairs to establish an earlier summer cutoff date for admission to the university so that student demand for classes could be assessed in a more timely way and extra sessions could be scheduled to meet demand. The vice-chancellor also requested that each dean provide a representative on site to meet with students who encountered special problems during the drop/add process.

As a direct response to student satisfaction survey findings, one dean took immediate steps to improve advising and to make adjustments that would give more students access to required courses. A full-time adviser for freshmen and sophomores was added to the dean's staff, and the average number of advisees assigned to each faculty member was reduced. Faculty in one department sought to improve the quality of information about its program by designing and distributing a new curriculum-planning sheet for majors.

Faculty and administrators in two colleges and a department in a third college were so concerned by SSS results for their students that they undertook follow-up surveys of their own for the purpose of gaining more specific information about their students' perceptions. The departmental faculty administered a modified version of the SSS instrument to the 1,100 students enrolled in all classes during the fall quarter. This procedure yielded comparative information on the teaching effectiveness of all faculty and graduate teaching assistants. The department head used this information in counseling with individual faculty and in designing appropriate group faculty development experiences. Other findings suggested that the department's introductory course should be restructured; this action is now being considered.

Early in 1984, the SSS instrument was administered by mail to a representative universitywide sample of 400 students and to appropriate samples of majors in six departments in five of the nine undergraduate colleges. The six departments (journalism; sociology; management; art and music education; geology; and forestry, wildlife, and fisheries) were selected because they were scheduled to undergo a comprehensive program review during 1984 or 1985, and the SSS information was intended to be included in the self-study prepared prior to the intensive peer review sessions. Some of the actions undertaken in response to the survey results were initiated by department heads, some by entire faculties functioning as a group, and some by specialized committees of faculty.

In three of the six departments, students indicated some dissatisfaction with internship experiences. For two of the three departments, this finding led to further exploration of student concerns and to subsequent improvement of existing programs. In the third department, no formal field experience was included in the curriculum at the time of the survey. The undergraduate curriculum committee of that department has been charged with responsibility for developing a field component for the program.

Student dissatisfaction with the quality of lower-division course work in the major led one department to redesign its introductory course. The responsible faculty committee has tried in its words to make the course "more relevant and interesting." Putting information from the SSS together with the experience of using a comprehensive exam for seniors, this department instituted a requirement that majors complete a sequence of five core courses by the end of the junior year.

In a department in which the head regularly conducts exit interviews with seniors, SSS responses provided some new directions for discussion: Now, specific questions are asked about the organization of the curriculum and the quality of courses in preparing for employment.

In the most tangible and immediately effective illustration of the use of outcomes information to date, the executive vice-chancellor has inserted a reference to the use of student outcome information as evidence of program quality in the instructions for use by program heads in preparing their annual budget requests. The information on freshman and senior COMP exam scores, accompanied by preliminary analyses of correlates of achievement in general education, including reasons given by freshmen for choosing to attend UTK, has been considered by the Planning and Budgeting Coordinating Committee as it seeks ways of clarifying the university's mission statement and communicating it to the clientele that the institution hopes to serve. The committee has begun to use the academic program review documents, with their new emphasis on student outcomes information, in making decisions about program mix and the allocation of internal resources. Finally, student outcomes were used as one criterion for the selection of campus proposals to be entered in Governor Lamar Alexander's 1984 statewide Centers of Excellence competition. In the past, the criteria for assessing quality in such procedures as these had been limited to input and process variables.

Implications for Other Settings

Program heads in all colleges at UTK are beginning to use outcomes data to inform the processes of teaching, advising, and improving curricula. Central administrators in the student affairs and business, planning, and finance divisions as well as in academic affairs are considering outcomes data as they make strategic decisions about program mix and the allocation of internal resources.

Collecting and analyzing outcomes information can be expensive. Thus, an institution must have a compelling reason to undertake these activities. Several motivating factors are present in higher education today: The need to demonstrate and improve program quality, to furnish evidence of accountability, to define a unique mission, to bolster declining enrollment through effective recruitment and retention strategies, and to evaluate the effectiveness of innovations.

Given both the motivation and the resources needed to embark on an assessment program, a successful effort requires that four other factors be present in the campus environment: leadership, technical support, communication, and time. At UTK, the chancellor, provost, and executive vice-chancellor have endorsed the instructional evaluation program and support it with essential funding. The academic deans have welcomed the addition of outcomes information to their sources of data for use in program evaluation. The deans have been instrumental in encouraging program heads to involve faculties in selecting or developing comprehensive exams and in using the results of testing and opinion surveys to improve their programs.

The placement of leadership for instructional evaluation in the academic affairs division of the university, with faculty playing key roles, has been an important factor in establishing the credibility of the program with deans, department heads, and other faculty. The Learning Research Center does not have the technical expertise or the access to student records needed to carry out the program independently. As a result, the center has forged strong links with the offices of institutional research, student data analysis, and information management systems so that center staff can use the institution's best resources for data storage and retrieval. Relying on existing units for service is less costly than creating new capacity for exclusive use in outcomes assessment, but good communications with the suppliers of services are essential if this strategy is to work efficiently and effectively.

Open, functioning channels of communication are all-important in the effort to collect and disseminate the results of outcomes studies. Faculty and even clerical staff in academic offices must be informed of the purposes of assessment so that they will be prepared to encourage students to take part in testing and opinion surveys. Staff in support offices must understand the services that are required for the assessment and the priority that they should receive. Student affairs and academic administrators and the faculty who must make the eventual improvements in programs and services must be quite familiar with the purposes and methods of assessment, and they should be involved to some extent in the selection or design of the instruments. At UTK, communication of the purposes and priorities associated with outcomes assessment has been initiated by the chancellor, the provost, and the executive vice-chancellor for business, planning, and finance.

Last, the kind of multifaceted outcomes assessment program now under way at UTK is a complex undertaking that takes time to put into place. Many individuals and offices must be convinced that such an effort is worth the time and expense that it entails. At UTK, the NCHEMS/ Kellogg project, with strong support from the chancellor and his staff, gave the institution time to step back from the THEC instructional evaluation initiative and view it from the perspective of the value that it could have for the institution.

After much study and discussion, the faculty-administrator task forces recommended that UTK should do more than simply comply with the THEC standards to qualify for performance funding. Instead, they felt that the university should adopt a proactive stance toward the standards and use them as the impetus for a serious institutionwide effort to apply student outcomes information in program evaluation and in program improvement and planning. Central administrators were receptive and took the steps necessary to prepare the campus community for a comprehensive data collection program that strongly emphasized dissemination and use of findings. Such leadership promotes communication, neutralizes potential opposition, and ensures that the technical and intellectual support needed for a successful student outcome assessment program is forthcoming.

References

Forrest, A. *Increasing Student Competence and Persistence: The Best Case for General Education.* Iowa City, Iowa: ACT National Center for the Advancement of Educational Practices, 1982.

Tennessee Higher Education Commission. *Instructional Evaluation Variables.* Nashville: Tennessee Higher Education Commission, 1983.

Winter, D., McClelland, D., and Stewart, A. *A New Case for the Liberal Arts: Assessing Institutional Goals and Student Development.* San Francisco: Jossey-Bass, 1981.

Trudy W. Banta is research professor in the University of Tennessee, Knoxville. Her responsibilities include coordination of the university's efforts to collect and use data about student learning and development in the context of Tennessee's performance-funding program.

At a critical point in one university's history, a
value-added student assessment model was developed.
Data generated by the model have been used to improve
student learning and development throughout the
curriculum, and they have helped the university to
clarify and revitalize its mission.

Using Outcomes Assessment: A Case Study in Institutional Change

Charles J. McClain
Darrell W. Krueger

Since the early 1970s, Northeast Missouri State University, an institution of 7,000 students located in outstate Missouri, has faced the need to operate in the context of a changing mission. The university was emerging from a tradition common to old normal schools, since it had been established primarily to produce teachers for northeast Missouri; in 1970, it faced the problem of expanding its mission to become a small multipurpose university.

As a teacher's college, the direction of the institution was well established. The rich tradition of the college inspired students, faculty, and staff with confidence in its soundness. Academic and nonacademic decisions had direction, and they were measured against commonly agreed on principles and practices. People at the college felt that they knew what had to be done in order to produce good teachers. Faculty and staff could verify how well they were doing by the placement of graduates, by feedback from principals and superintendents who had hired graduates, and by the intimate working relationships that the college had developed with the public

P. T. Ewell (Ed.). *Assessing Educational Outcomes*. New Directions
for Institutional Research, no. 47. San Francisco: Jossey-Bass, September 1985.

schools. Obstacles to success were well understood, largely agreed on, and thoroughly debated.

In becoming a comprehensive university, students, faculty, and staff faced the problem of establishing confidence in the academic and nonacademic decisions they were making. In bringing about a mission change of this magnitude, faculty and staff had problems even in identifying the obstacles to success. New traditions needed to be established to create a fresh sense of direction and a new momentum as the teacher's college became a multipurpose university. In many new areas of study, the institution needed to discover what had to be done in order to produce qualified graduates. Determining how well the university was doing in producing nationally competitive graduates was critical in establishing a reputation of quality in many diverse fields.

The problem of adjusting to a change in mission is not unique to Northeast Missouri State University. Indeed, it has been experienced by most if not all institutions in the American Association of State Colleges and Universities. The manner in which Northeast Missouri State University approached this challenge and the role of outcomes assessment in the process are the subjects of this chapter.

Design of the Assessment

The need to find solutions to the problems emerging from the change in university mission gave impetus to Northeast Missouri State University's outcomes assessment model. From the outset, solutions were sought from within a strong empirical context. There was a need to know everything possible about the university. As a result, plans were developed to build financial, faculty, alumni, and student data bases. Because the primary purpose of the university was student learning, the foundation for assessments of the university's effectiveness became the student data system. And, the student was looked at from a point of view that emphasized his or her whole academic and social life. The student's academic and cocurricular growth were both considered important, and they needed to be analyzed as part of assessment. Thus, a conceptual system was developed at the very beginning to identify critical points in the student's experience at Northeast. This system determined what kinds of data were needed to analyze the impact of the university at each point. It was embodied in a flow chart that tracked the student's experience at the university (Figure 1). This chart served to organize and coordinate many distinct data collection efforts. After the contact points had been outlined, a second chart was developed that summarized the data elements to be observed at each point in time (Figure 2). This chart served as an actual blueprint for data collection.

The theoretical model for the student data base outlined in Figures

Figure 1. University/Student Contacts

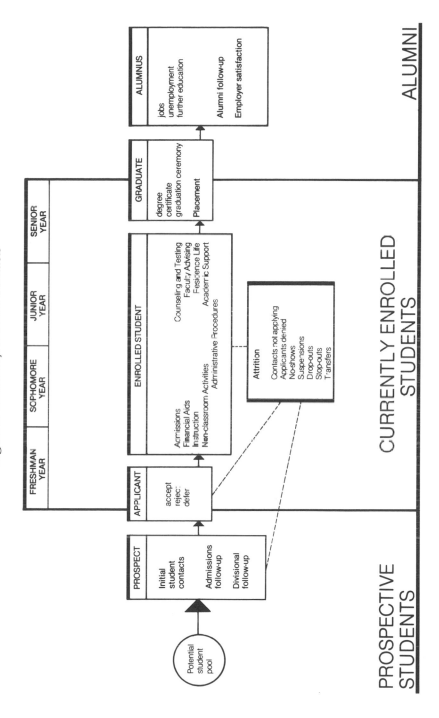

Figure 2. Student Data Record

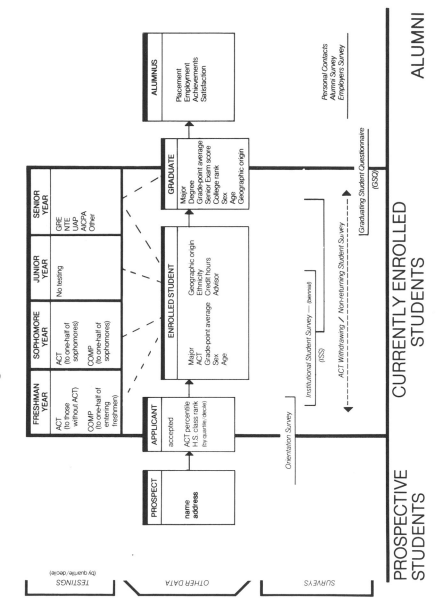

1 and 2 in fact predated the university's ability to collect and store large amounts of information. Fortunately, the university assembled the comprehensive theoretical model before the data collection and computer systems were available to implement what Northeast felt it was important to know and understand about students. Thus, as computerized storage capability was developed and data collection points were added, the model became increasingly sophisticated in its collection, analysis, and dissemination of data. Throughout the process, the theoretical model both directed and expanded the long-range potential of the university's outcomes assessment effort.

Early thinking about what Northeast actually wanted to be able to demonstrate through outcomes assessment emphasized the concept that the university experience should make a positive difference in each student's knowledge, attitudes, and skills (Astin, 1968, 1982). As a result, although only a portion of the eventual data collection system could be tied directly to the assessment of change, the total outcomes assessment model has been loosely referred to (both on and off campus) as a value-added model. However, it has been just as important to demonstrate that students who graduate from Northeast Missouri State University are nationally competitive as it has been to demonstrate that the university has had a positive influence on students. One portion of the assessment system was explicitly constructed to serve that objective. Thus, three primary goals were fundamental in developing the outcomes data collection system: the desire to know everything possible about the student, the wish to demonstrate that the university made a positive difference in the student's life, and the desire to demonstrate that students who graduated from the university were nationally competitive.

Data Elements

Given the three goals just outlined, three types of data were identified as critical to the student record system. First, standard demographic data elements—gender, geographic origin, race or ethnicity, high school class rank, entering test scores, grade point average, major, and adviser— were identified as essential. Most institutions collect such data on a regular basis, and at Northeast they constitute a base that can be used to analyze various kinds of outcomes data. Second, ability and achievement measures were sought from national standardized tests. The intention was to measure student achievement in both the major and the general education program. Third, the university wanted to find out about students' attitudes and development.

In the major, the university wanted to compare the strength of its students and programs with students and programs elsewhere in the country. Faculty were asked to identify tests that they felt best met this goal. In most cases, their response was the national examination commonly used in their field. As a result, the university has been giving standardized examinations to graduating seniors since 1973. At present, these exams include the Graduate Record Exmination field tests, the National Teacher Examination, the American Institute of Certified Public Accountants (AICPA) Level II Achievement Exam, and Undergraduate Assessment Program (UAP) area examinations. In areas where no national exam is available, local senior exams have been developed.

In general education, the university wanted to assess the impact that it was having in mathematics and in English and, as tests became available, in other areas of general education as well. Thus, beginning in 1975, the Sequential Tests for Educational Progress were adopted. In 1978 the American College Testing (ACT) program entrance examination—already taken by most entering freshmen—began to be regularly readministered to sophomores. Currently, all students are retested on the ACT test and some on the ACT College Outcome Measures Project assessment tests at the end of the sophomore year.

In order to observe student attitudes and development, a systematic set of surveys was designed. Students are currently surveyed about their educational goals, their choice of college, their overall perceptions of the university, and their progress toward specific educational outcomes and toward the university's general education objectives. Questionnaires are administered at four points: at freshman orientation, during the time when the student is enrolled at the university, as a graduating senior, and as an alumnus.

As a result of these surveys, the university can trace changes in the perceptions of individual students over time. By maintaining longitudinal data and by using the same questions in readministrations of the survey over the years, the university is developing profiles of change in student perceptions of university programs and services. These surveys have been administered since 1975; they were redesigned in recent years to ensure that parallel data were collected with each questionnaire. Most questions have been adopted because they explicitly measure particular university goals. Many questions are original; others have resulted from reviews of ACT, National Center for Higher Education Management Systems, and other national surveys. Although largely homegrown, the surveys thus reflect the data collection practices of established national surveys. Since the questionnaires have been conducted for a relatively long period of time, they have become extremely helpful in assessing the university's effectiveness.

Data Analysis

Because the data system is so extensive, analysis has proved a challenge. Outcomes data have been examined primarily through observation of trends in individual data elements, such as sophomore test score gains or enrolled students' attitudes toward the institution. Then, by using percentages or mean scores, individual student, program, discipline (department), division (school), and universitywide results can be compared with comparable results over time, with one another, and, where data are available, with national norms.

At each level of analysis, a different set of questions is asked about the relative importance of the data and about whether the achievement meets expected or desirable levels. Many faculty first make a naive assumption that individual discipline or divisional results will be similar to universitywide data. Variances in unit results from universitywide averages raise explicit questions about the scores on particular tests for particular populations. Seeking answers to these questions often leads to important curriculum changes, alterations in course content, or general program improvements. If the data obtained are either better or worse than expected, possible explanations are developed and then tested. More sophisticated analysis of the data can be conducted at this point to explore these differences.

At Northeast, there is a strong feeling that outcomes data should be placed in the hands of the people who make the decisions. Initially, results of assessment studies are broadly shared to ensure accuracy and to promote use. A broad-based review helps to detect problems in data collection or computer programming at an early point. Collection, analysis, and dissemination of information are coordinated by the dean of instruction, and the data are sent directly to division heads, faculty, and other interested persons for further analysis and interpretation. Accessible data give faculty and division heads valuable information and enable them to have or to secure control over their own destinies.

The Results of Assessment

Assessment has had an impressive influence on Northeast Missouri State University. The university's assessment program not only created the conditions for change, but it also helped to give direction and substance to needed change. The university has been able to build on selected portions of its heritage and take incremental steps guided by evaluation toward a new, high-quality small public university with demonstrated excellence in selected fields.

The comprehensive outcomes data system has acted as a catalyst for decision making. The assessment program has created an environment emphasizing the essential mission of higher education, namely, the education and achievement of students. It has increased attention on campus to the quality of education as a priority, and emphasis on the size of enrollment has decreased (Enthoven, 1970). This refocusing seems to have improved faculty morale. It has increased faculty awareness of national expectations for university graduates and the comparative strength of our graduates in the job market after graduation. It has provoked discussion about student satisfaction with university services. It has reinforced the value of general education and promoted reexamination and strengthening of the general education curriculum. It has prompted a reevaluation of university academic policies. It has created conditions prompting the commissioner of higher education to recommend a mission change that recognizes the nationally competitive quality of the student body. Finally, it has directed the attention of publics outside the university to the university's demonstrated performance.

Many cases can be cited to show the benefits of outcomes assessment data in helping decision makers to evaluate the accomplishments of distinctly different programs. Cases involving the use of sophomore test data, senior test data, and survey data are particularly illustrative of the process.

The first case involves the use of sophomore test results. At Northeast, the ACT test has been readministered to sophomores for five consecutive years. Sophomore scores are compared with the scores of incoming freshman in order to determine the degree of change that has occurred. As Figure 3 shows, the results for the period between 1978 and 1983 were mixed. After seeing these results, faculty expressed concern about the test score gains of sophomores in mathematics. Business faculty were the first to take an interest in seeing whether sophomore ACT mathematics scores could be improved, since their students were not showing achievement in mathematics at an appropriate level. In fact, no improvement was shown, and in several cases scores actually declined. After careful study, faculty decided to direct business students toward more appropriate math courses. Thus, mathematical analysis or finite mathematics was recommended for the mathematics general education requirement. Subsequently, the mathematics scores of sophomore business administration students began to improve on the ACT test (Figure 4).

When evidence of business students' score changes began to be discussed on campus, pressure grew to require college algebra of all students. The math faculty were divided on this issue. Some felt that most students were not prepared for college algebra. Others felt that an existing contemporary mathematics course, which was designed to deepen students' appreciation of mathematics, not to teach mathematics, better fulfilled the philosophy and objectives of general education. Still others debated the appropriateness of using ACT scores to measure the university's influence on students' knowledge of mathematics and the appropriateness of using norm-referenced tests as a measure. After considerable debate, the mathematics faculty recommended that all students have at least college algebra. In making this recommendation, math faculty did not resolve the issue of the appropriateness of the ACT test. The recommendation was based instead on what faculty felt would best help students. When the recom-

Figure 3. ACT Percentile Change Study; Freshman Year vs. Sophomore Year University Summary; (Five Years by Subtest and Composite)

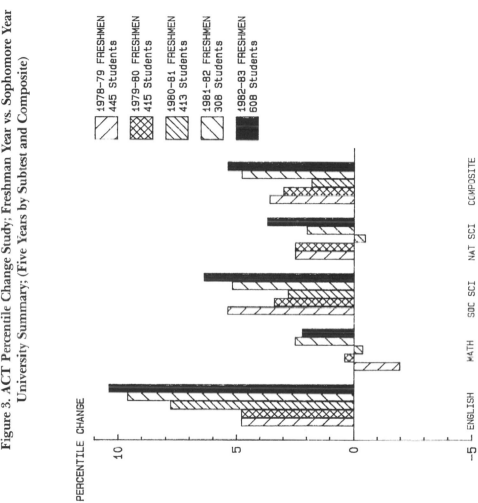

Figure 4. Math ACT Percentile Change Study; Freshmen vs. Sophomores University Total vs. Business Administration; Five Years by Math Subtest

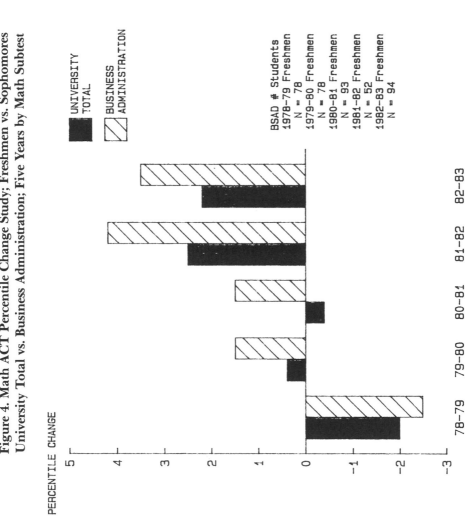

mendation went forward to the faculty committees, it was overwhelmingly supported. There is every expectation that students will now be better prepared to deal with mathematical problems and mathematical issues when they graduate.

The change in the performance of accounting students on the AICPA test was even more dramatic. Since 1973, accounting students at Northeast had been taking the UAP exam in business. In 1980, the faculty decided that the UAP was not the appropriate national exam for accounting majors and recommended that it be replaced by the AICPA Level II Achievement Exam. On the first testing in 1981, 47 percent of the accounting majors scored above the fiftieth percentile. Although the test was normed against a select sample of accounting professionals, faculty were not satisfied with the overall achievement level of their students as measured by the examination. They carefully studied the curriculum and student ability against particular patterns of test score results. Changes were made in the curriculum, and several accounting courses were made more rigorous. Discussions with students whose achievements did not meet expectations led faculty to try to increase the long-term memory of specific course content by requiring comprehensive final exams in more classes. Additional credentialed faculty were hired. Probably as a result of these changes, 57 percent of the 1984 class scored above the fiftieth percentile on the AICPA senior exam, a ten percentile gain in just four years.

Survey data have helped to improve the university in many other ways. For example, the 1980–81 graduating student questionnaire showed that students had a relatively negative attitude toward freshman counseling. However, steps had already been taken to change the direction of freshman counseling. These steps included increasing the emphasis on summer orientation, improving advisement of undecided students, and adding a career-planning component to the freshman counseling system. By setting clearly defined goals, by focusing on students who were high persisters, and by building informal meetings between counselors and students into the freshman counseling schedule, the freshman counseling program has been improved: Graduating seniors have expressed a progressively more positive attitude toward freshman counseling.

The fourth example concerns the use of performance measures in the university's budget request. In fall 1979, the Missouri Department of Higher Education, along with the Governor's Office of Budget and Planning, asked each institution to suggest items for funding that were specifically designed to improve the quality of their programs. There was strong support at the state level for experimentation with a funding scheme that rewarded quality. This support was based on a recognition that enrollment-driven formulas rewarded quantitative input measures, not the actual educational product.

In response to the request, Northeast submitted a modest performance-based improvement request, with appropriate measurements attached. The request was funded for $407,868—about 48 percent of the amount requested. The actual program request followed a logical sequence that began with the university mission, moved to specific goals that needed to be accomplished, and outlined how the university measures the success attained in achieving the goals. The request itself focused on objectives in the general education program and in the major field. Specific performance goals were established for the sophomore test, for the senior test, and for selected items on the student surveys. A program for attaining each goal was outlined. Finally, appropriate estimates of the dollar amounts needed to implement each goal were provided.

The university's academic divisions also submitted program improvement requests following the format just outlined. Each division identified its role in fulfilling the university mission, proposed action strategies for achieving stated goals, determined appropriate measures of goal achievement, developed tactics for achieving goals, and specified the estimated dollar amount deemed necessary to implement the outlined program.

State funding for a portion of this request strongly reinforced the emphasis on quality then emerging on campus. More faculty paid attention to the results—especially faculty whose positions were funded with money that came through the request. Ultimately, however, the money was not as important as the external recognition for the university's willingness to measure results.

In fiscal year 1985, the university's program improvement request was funded in the amount of $478,000. Again, this recognition had a great impact on the university. Support for specific improvements aimed at meeting the outcome goals outlined in the request has intensified. Repeated recognition continues to result in measurable improvements in actual performance.

Future of Outcomes Assessment

Faculty and staff have generally supported the survey portion of the assessment model, especially since the surveys have been revised and the questionnaires have been updated. At first, many at the university were quite skeptical about the cognitive testing program. As at other colleges and universities, some questioned the nature of the tests, the norms of the test, the actual motivation of students in taking the tests, the analysis of test results, and the potential harm of teaching directly to the tests (Austin and Garber, 1982). However, as time went on and as answers to some of these questions were found, more people at the university gained confidence in the testing model. The legitimacy of the testing portion of outcomes assessment has grown as its importance to the university has increased.

Many of those who initially questioned the data have recognized the importance of outcomes assessment in communicating the university's concern about quality to both students and external constituencies. From demonstrating concern about quality and using the data to monitor, re-evaluate, and judge effectiveness, many programs have moved to a point where assessment results confirm and substantiate the achievement and performance level of their students. Thus, value-added assessment has confirmed institutional quality. In sum, the symbolic value of the model in demonstrating the university's concern about quality has helped to produce changes in many programs, where year after year senior test scores are high, sophomore scores indicate meaningful gains in performance beyond expected levels, or both. Some might argue that continued success means that it is no longer necessary to measure outcomes. But, constant, careful product evaluation can be very helpful in anticipating changes in the composition of the program or the student body. Furthermore, techniques of analysis and data collection, as well as improvements in survey and test instruments, should persuade most to continue the assessment process, especially as explanations for individual student achievement or nonachievement are found.

Summary and Recommendations

The outcomes assessment program has been central in helping Northeast Missouri State University bring about significant institutional change (Northeast Missouri State University, 1984). The program began with a desire to build a comprehensive data base about the university. In this process, outcomes measures, such as sophomore and senior test scores, along with student survey data became basic elements of the data base. Comparison of student, program, and divisional assessment results with national and universitywide norms has enabled the university to monitor strengths and weaknesses. Significant decision-making guidance has been one result of an assessment process that has brought about a more productive and higher-quality university. The future of the assessment program looks very positive. Its legitimacy has been established, and its success has been recognized. In a time when the pressure for external evaluation of colleges and universities is intensifying, the assessment program should guarantee that the image of the university is enhanced and substantiated.

The suggestions that follow are offered to institutions that wish to implement an outcomes assessment program:

- Put together a theoretical construct conceptualizing the needed data items, levels of analysis, and purposes of the model
- Use all the data presently available, for example, demographic data, results from national tests, such as the Law School Admission Test and Medical College Admission Test, and any survey data already collected

- Begin collecting the desired data elements, using data that are easy to understand and communicate
- Give all levels of the university access to the data
- Analyze the data by organizational units, that is, by discipline, college, and university
- Let the data themselves raise the important questions, and use the data to reward the achievers
- Focus attention on strengthening weak areas revealed by the data, not on eliminating them
- Finally, keep in mind that universities are about learning and that assessment data are of value only if they are used to support the learning process.

References

Astin, A. W. "Undergraduate Achievement and Institutional 'Excellence.'" *Science,* 1968, *161,* 661-667.

Astin, A. W. "Why Not Try Some New Ways of Measuring Quality?" *Educational Record,* 1982, *63,* 10-15.

Austin, G. R., and Garber, H. (Eds.). *The Rise and Fall of Test Scores.* New York: Academic Press, 1982.

Enthoven, A. C. "Measures of the Outputs of Higher Education: Some Practical Suggestions for Their Development and Use." In B. Lawrence, G. Weathersby, and V. W. Patterson (Eds.), *Outputs of Higher Education: Their Identification, Measurements, and Evaluation.* Boulder, Colo.: Western Interstate Commission for Higher Education, 1970.

Northeast Missouri State University. *In Pursuit of Degrees with Integrity: A Value-Added Approach to Undergraduate Assessment.* Washington, D.C.: American Association of State Colleges and Universities, 1984.

Charles J. McClain is president of Northeast Missouri State University. He conceived and implemented the value-added assessment program at that institution.

Darrell W. Krueger is dean of instruction at Northeast Missouri State University. His office directs the value-added assessment program.

*A multifaceted assessment process allows the
development of each student to be observed and
improved as she moves through the curriculum. A
corresponding evaluation process allows the content
of curricula to be validated against external, real-world
standards.*

Assessing and Validating the Outcomes of College

*Marcia Mentkowski
Georgine Loacker*

Alverno College is a liberal arts college for women with a strong focus on
preparing its students for professional careers. It presently serves more than
1,500 degree students, who attend Alverno on both weekdays and weekends.
Accountability for student outcomes is centered in the values of the college.
Some of the liberal learning values that Alverno faculty intend to transmit
to their students and that they model through its curriculum are active self-
sustained learning, involvement in learning, individual development and
change, realization of human potential and self-assessment, application of
knowledge, and achievement of competence and efficacy. In 1973, the
faculty forcefully expressed these values by designing a new curriculum in
which all students had to demonstrate certain major abilities within their
disciplines or professional areas in order to graduate. These abilities
included communication, analysis, problem solving, valuing, social interaction, taking environmental responsibility, involvement in the contemporary world, and esthetic response (Alverno College Faculty, 1976).

In the process of defining these abilities, the faculty realized that
students would be more likely to develop self-sustained learning if they
participated in a process that tested these abilities individually and directly.

P. T. Ewell (Ed.). *Assessing Educational Outcomes*. New Directions
for Institutional Research, no. 47. San Francisco: Jossey-Bass, September 1985.

47

The faculty subsequently designed an institutionwide measurement system to measure each student's progress in developing her abilities, to give each student diagnostic feedback, and to certify that each student had achieved these abilities for graduation. This system constituted a first approach to assessment of student outcomes (Alverno College Faculty, 1979).

In 1976, the faculty created an Office of Research and Evaluation to establish research and evaluation as a curricular component. The purpose of the office was to evaluate the quality, effectiveness, and validity of the curriculum, to establish the validity of college-learned abilities for lifelong learning, and to inform theory and practice in student learning and development. (The college also carries out traditional institutional research work in its administrative offices to assist in college governance policy and planning.)

The studies undertaken by the office to validate the effectiveness of Alverno's curriculum constitute a second approach to student outcomes assessment (Mentkowski and Doherty, 1983, 1984). The purpose of this chapter is to explore these two expanded approaches to accountability for student outcomes. The chapter will describe how these approaches work and the benefits that have accrued to students and the college after twelve years.

The First Approach: Assessing Individual Student Performance

A complex individual assessment process is central to Alverno's ability-based curriculum. The faculty create criteria or descriptive statements that give a picture of each ability to be assessed. Then they design instruments to elicit evidence of that ability in each student. To judge students' performance, faculty, students, and external assessors from the Milwaukee professional and business communities use the criteria to determine what aspects of an ability a student has already developed and which need further attention.

Assumptions and Components of Assessment. Assessment design flows from a series of important assumptions about learning and its relation to assessment. For example, faculty believe that learning involves a change in behavior. Learning includes development of abilities that incorporate, apply, and extend knowledge. Learning is enhanced when the learner sets out to achieve explicit goals.

The faculty also assume that assessment can describe and judge the level of learning that an individual has reached. At the same time, assessment can contribute to learning by making goals and criteria explicit and by eliciting behaviors that demonstrate and exercise an ability. Furthermore, any attempt to assess an ability increases understanding of it for teachers and students (Loacker and others, 1984; Early and others, 1980).

The assessment process built on these assumptions is depicted in Figure 1. It has six components. First, the ability that constitutes the learn-

Figure 1. Components of the Assessment Process

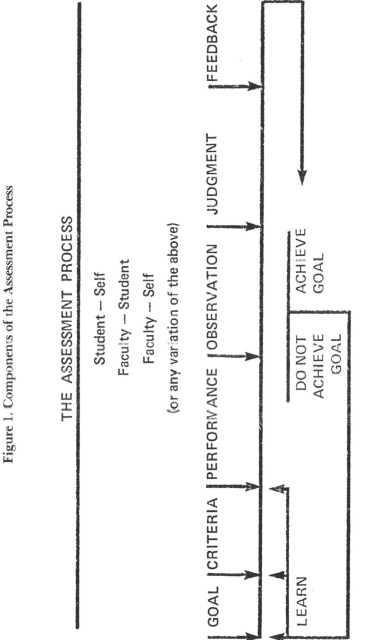

THE ASSESSMENT PROCESS

Student — Self

Faculty — Student

Faculty — Self

(or any variation of the above)

GOAL | CRITERIA | PERFORMANCE | OBSERVATION | JUDGMENT | FEEDBACK

LEARN

DO NOT ACHIEVE GOAL

ACHIEVE GOAL

ing goal must be explicit. Second, explicit criteria describe the ability. Third, the student provides a sample performance. Fourth, careful observation of the performance and application of the criteria lead, fifth, to expert judgment and, sixth, to feedback that provides the student with information on the strengths and weaknesses of the performance. Underlying the process are multiple judgments across contexts, self-assessment or judgment by the student assessor, appropriate levels of externality, and certification of the ability.

Characteristics of Assessment. The assessment process is designed to provide assurance that the abilities that a student shows are at some point becoming personalized—part of her habitual way of handling situations. To accomplish that purpose, assessment instruments are designed to contribute to a process that is generic, developmental, and holistic.

First, because the abilities that Alverno students are required to develop are generic, the assessment process must cumulatively focus on abilities that are not simply specific to a particular task or situation. Abilities must be transferred and modified in various situations. Thus, assessments administered to students must be both external and multiple. Externality appears in several ways and to varied degrees. For example, the criteria used to assess a given ability level can be developed by department members outside a particular course setting. The instruments used or developed can involve content across courses or disciplines. Assessors themselves are often drawn from outside the classroom and from off campus. Multiplicity occurs by requiring a single ability to be validated in several settings and by using multiple viewpoints—instructors and faculty coassessors, off-campus assessors, peers, and self-assessment. The use of multiple assessments gives the student the opportunity and the obligation to seek certification in a variety of settings.

Second, the faculty approach student abilities in developmental ways. This means not only that ability levels are sequenced in a progressive learning pattern but that assessment itself becomes a teaching tool. Faculty make assessment a teaching tool by making assessment techniques and criteria public and explicit and by presenting the results to students immediately, in detail, in a structured feedback situation.

At the beginning of each course, the instructor spells out the course goals in the syllabus, including the ability levels that a student should be ready to demonstrate as a result of the course experience. In the syllabus, the instructor relates particular course materials and assignments to the goals of the course. The syllabus specifies the assessment techniques to be used and enumerates the criteria on which students' work will be judged. During the course, each student receives ongoing assessment. Ongoing assessment gives both student and instructor a diagnostic view of the student's learning progress. As soon as possible after each assessment, the student receives detailed feedback on her performance as regards the overall course goals and the specific criteria set forth in the syllabus.

Whether the assessment situation is as simple as a series of one-paragraph responses to questions about a film, or as complex as presenting a park-use plan to a neighborhood association, faculty try to use it as a learning experience. Ideally, assessment should foster a process of working toward explicit, known goals, with frequent stops to determine the state of the art in the ability that the student is working to develop.

Finally, student abilities are in reality holistic; they are parts of the whole person. Sequential levels of abilities are therefore cumulative in both experience and assessment. Each level builds on and includes the preceding levels, and the student has frequent opportunities to further evaluate and refine abilities that have already been credentialed. Indeed, faculty constantly coordinate instructional efforts to ensure that this occurs automatically.

At the same time, learning and assessment look beyond the level at hand. In each course or individual learning experience and in each assessment situation, faculty attempt to elicit the most advanced possible performance from students. That the possibilities for exhibiting competence are unlimited is most evident at the advanced levels. There, students help to design or select highly complex assessment situations, often in professional or other field settings, that challenge their abilities to their fullest. In recording exact information about a student's performance, assessors may be called on to judge whether a given element is present or absent, to quantify its frequency, or to use a rating scale. Always, they are expected to note illustrative examples. However, in both qualitative and quantitative measures, faculty take care not to place a ceiling on the degree to which a student may excel in demonstrating the criteria involved.

That abilities and their assessment are integrated by nature is, again, most apparent at the advanced levels. Early assessments are fairly well enclosed in their design in order to focus the student's attention on a particular element of a single ability. However, by the time a student is working at advanced levels, faculty are looking explicitly at several abilities operating in concert.

Insistence on a holistic focus has helped to remind faculty of the surprising variety of ways in which a given ability can be demonstrated. The students' myriad variations on the theme set by a given instrument continually broaden faculty awareness of what to look for as well as provide concrete evidence of students' own unique, developing styles. Assessors are thus enabled to appreciate a wide range of definitions for successful performance. They also learn more about how to design assessment experiences, fine-tune them for specificity, and open them to elicit the richest possible response.

The design of instruments to assess all levels of student abilities within and across all disciplines has become a major creative work for Alverno faculty. Instruments include live and videotaped work samples from science labs or the classrooms of student teachers. They include written and oral samples of thinking, such as logs or reflective presentations. Individual and group simulations, ranging from simple written exercises and short case studies to complex organizational situations that extend to a week and beyond, are especially valuable. Such assessments require students to apply their knowledge, gather new data, and solve complex problems appropriate to their discipline. Faculty continually review their own and each other's instruments to ensure that all assessment components are present and that the performances elicited and the criteria identified provide a credible picture of the ability to be demonstrated.

Responsibility for Assessment. The work of monitoring assessment techniques for comparability and of developing collegewide instruments and criteria that assess abilities across disciplines is a major responsibility of the Assessment Committee. This body, which has representatives for each ability, the Assessment Center, the Office of Research and Evaluation, and related support areas, is charged with overseeing the entire assessment system as it evolves. This work is carried on simultaneously in several other areas as well. It is a continuing part of the collaborative work of each academic and professional department and of the Discipline Divisions into which the departments are organized. Each of the eight interdisciplinary divisions representing the eight abilities also has a major responsibility to review assessment techniques across disciplines.

The Assessment Committee's most important responsibility is constantly to rethink goals and to seek out and nurture any promising new avenues of inquiry or insight. Just as the interdisciplinary divisions do with individual abilities, committee members work constantly to pull together what faculty have learned about assessment and its contribution to learning and about ways of altering or augmenting the overall assessment system.

Benefits of Assessment. The intended function of the individual assessment process is to provide each student with diagnostic information on her progress in developing abilities, to contribute to the progress itself, and to credential each student's performance. However, assessment can also be used to improve the curriculum and establish its internal validity.

First, data on individual student performance in the assessment process are a major way of determining whether teaching and assessment designs for learning are actually working and for whom. Such data can be examined as a part of course evaluation. Thus, general and specialized learning outcomes become the content of conversation within and across departments. Because all students and faculty participate in the assessment process and use its common language, learning becomes the stuff of discussion at many levels in the college. Both students and faculty can ask of each situation, Is this what we want to happen?

Participating in the assessment process has helped students to develop self-sustained learning (Mentkowski and Doherty, 1984). In confidential, longitudinal interviews, students attributed the ability to take responsibility for their own learning and to develop different ways of learning to feedback from faculty on their strengths and weaknesses in performance situations. Other factors that students and alumnae have identified as important are the opportunities for self-assessment—for judging their own performance against explicit criteria.

The assessment process is also clearly a benefit for faculty. Information on particular abilities and on how students perform them often leads faculty to revise assessment criteria or instruments. For example, the Valuing Department recently revised the descriptions of the valuing ability at the advanced levels. Faculty also report improved teaching strategies that are based on enhanced knowledge of individual differences in students' performance of an ability and of how students learn.

Finally, the assessment process is the best source of data for immediate day-to-day improvements in the curriculum. As student performance data become available, faculty have ways of judging how students are learning well before the end of the semester. They can adjust their teaching strategies accordingly, or they can redesign the assessments in order to elicit an ability better. Through the commitment to assessment and the constant generation of information on student learning, the assessment process keeps the institution focused on the development of student learning outcomes. The value that the institution places on learning about how to teach and on giving feedback on performance is constantly emphasized through the assessment process. Learning to assess is an important way in which new faculty become effective teachers. Learning to assess themselves is an important way in which students become effective learners.

The Second Approach: Validating Student Outcomes Across the Curriculum

In contrast to the individual assessment process, the evaluation and validation process, which is depicted in Figure 2, enables faculty to look at and intervene in the total program. Evaluation makes it possible to step back from the program objectively and systematically and to take a hard look at program functioning and at validity in terms of student and alumnae outcomes. Since 1976, many questions have been studied with support from Alverno College and from a three-year grant from the National Institute of Education (Mentkowski and Doherty, 1983).

Assumptions of Evaluation. Definitions of the validity of an educational program and evaluation designs intended to test this validity must be both built on and consistent with existing administrative structures and collegewide goals. The extent to which faculty use the results of evaluative activities to improve the curriculum is the ultimate test of these activities. It also mirrors the degree to which the college has been able to create an

Figure 2. A Description of Alverno Curriculum Components.

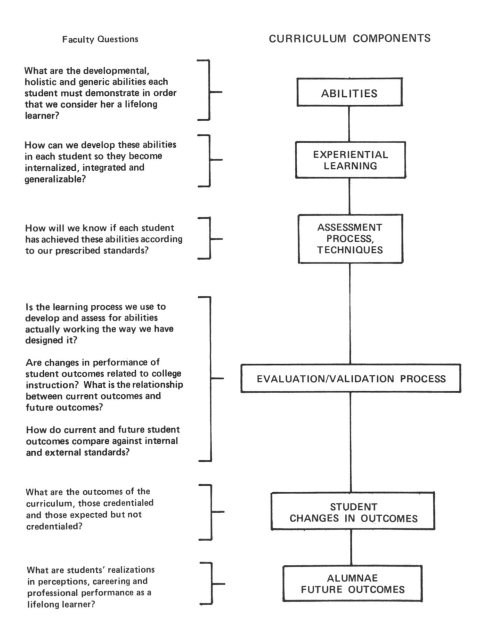

Faculty Questions

CURRICULUM COMPONENTS

What are the developmental, holistic and generic abilities each student must demonstrate in order that we consider her a lifelong learner?

ABILITIES

How can we develop these abilities in each student so they become internalized, integrated and generalizable?

EXPERIENTIAL LEARNING

How will we know if each student has achieved these abilities according to our prescribed standards?

ASSESSMENT PROCESS, TECHNIQUES

Is the learning process we use to develop and assess for abilities actually working the way we have designed it?

Are changes in performance of student outcomes related to college instruction? What is the relationship between current outcomes and future outcomes?

How do current and future student outcomes compare against internal and external standards?

EVALUATION/VALIDATION PROCESS

What are the outcomes of the curriculum, those credentialed and those expected but not credentialed?

STUDENT CHANGES IN OUTCOMES

What are students' realizations in perceptions, careering and professional performance as a lifelong learner?

ALUMNAE FUTURE OUTCOMES

effective practice-based research "laboratory" to ensure further program development.

Alverno researchers soon came to realize that they needed to rethink the concept of validity in light of the assumptions about assessment that are inherent in an ability-based curriculum. Establishing validity first meant defining its meaning and use in the Alverno context. The resulting rethinking identified two quite different concepts that could serve as the foundation for evaluation: design-based validity and performance-based validity.

Design-based validity refers to strategies that monitor program function and compare the program with standards set during program design. A program can be said to have design-based validity when comparison of what was intended with what is actually happening on a day-to-day basis indicates that the intention is being realized. The comparison is effected through a variety of review procedures. For example, the Assessment Committee evaluates individual instruments and course syllabi, and external assessors from the Milwaukee community judge student performance and critique the assessment process. Here is where the vast amounts of data generated by the assessment of individual student performance can be used to evaluate curricular effectiveness.

Performance-based validity refers to the strategy of researching actual student performances both during and beyond college. Validity rests on whether actual student performance changes over time as the result of instruction, whether these changes persist beyond college, and whether they show up on measures of abilities drawn from outside the college. To illustrate, let us suppose that a study of student performance shows a change on a faculty-designed measure of analytical thinking in management. Faculty ask, How does the range of performance compare with how we have defined the ability and, Is development of analytical thinking really the result of our instruction? They may also ask, How do students perform on a particular external criterion measure of analytical thinking? or, How would outstanding professionals in management who are not our graduates demonstrate analysis, and how do our alumnae show the beginnings of this ability on the job?

With design-based evaluation and validation strategies in place, research results from performance-based validation strategies are more likely to be incorporated into program development efforts. If a program is constantly changing and assessment techniques are consistently being revised, new information has a place to go—a place where it can begin to be used in a practical context.

Components of Evaluation. The foundation of any evaluation process is comparison. But, what should be the basis of the comparison? We select standards (What is it possible for students to achieve?) rather than norms (How do our students compare with students at other colleges?)

wherever possible (Popham, 1978). But, whose standards? And, what kind of standards are adequate? We have chosen the frameworks and measures that are most likely to meet our own standards and educational values. Yet, we recognize that choice or selection of any standard—whether a measure of cognitive development, a set of abilities that describe professional performance at work, a set of norms based on a range of student performance, advice from a group of external assessors, or goals from program designers—is somewhat arbitrary. We deal with this issue by using multiple sources: We use multiple approaches for establishing validity, we use multiple standards from sources both internal and external to the curriculum, and we use multiple measurement techniques, drawn from multiple theoretical frameworks, to measure our students' performance.

To meet this demand for multiplicity, we designed an evaluation model with four levels of triangulation. We also built externality into every level of the model so that findings could be used not only to improve a particular curriculum but also to generate findings that might generalize to teaching and learning settings and to populations at other institutions. The attention to externality also helps to solve the inherent problems of subjectivity that arise when a college takes on its own validation.

Since the findings from evaluation efforts should result in curriculum improvement, such models need to have a dynamic quality that fits an ever-changing curriculum. Classic experimental group–control group comparisons are not possible in settings where variables, treatment, and settings are constantly changing. Yet, the model must allow some examination of causal relationships between student outcomes and actual performance in the curriculum. This means that we must use longitudinal designs to measure change. Further, such models must generate group results that can influence curriculum and program development and shape the long-range policies of a college. Yet, they must also generate specific findings about patterns in individual differences and corresponding teaching strategies that work for individualized instruction. Altogether this means generating both individual and group results.

Finally, evaluation models must allow a series of findings from a range of data sources to emerge over time, since faculty need fast results if they are to solve curriculum problems that need immediate resolution. Yet, the need for long-range longitudinal designs and the complex effort needed to research some questions means waiting for results.

Alverno incorporates these evaluation components into a model that has four levels of triangulation; this model is depicted in Figure 3. We study abilities from multiple points of view, across multiple points in time, using multiple groups, and with multiple opportunities for critique and comparison against standards. As we widen the lens, we bring more comparisons into play in order to test our assumptions. We use longitudinal and cross sectional designs within the larger model to pinpoint change

Figure 3. The Triangulated Validation Model

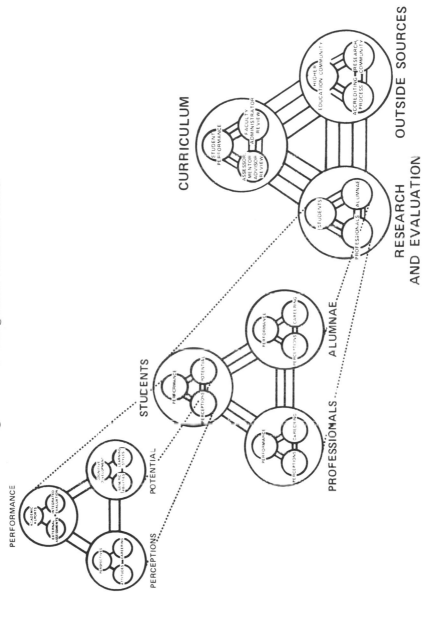

PERFORMANCE

POTENTIAL

PERCEPTIONS

STUDENTS

ALUMNAE

PROFESSIONALS

CURRICULUM

OUTSIDE SOURCES

RESEARCH
AND EVALUATION

and relate it to student performance in the curriculum from several perspectives. Further, the triangulated model allows us to make comparisons across various groups.

To date, the Office of Research and Evaluation has collected some 18,500 responses from 990 students, alumnae, and professionals. Two complete entering classes were studied throughout college, and 200 of these students formed the basis of our longitudinal comparisons. We used twenty-six measures drawn from six theoretical frameworks, and we conducted 400 confidential longitudinal interviews. The results, described in a series of twelve research reports, have been summarized by Mentkowski and Doherty (1983, 1984).

One picture of student abilities emerges from student performance on faculty-designed assessments. We enhance this picture by studying student perceptions through confidential interviews. Student growth on measures of human potential drawn from outside the college gives still another picture of student outcomes. Findings that are corroborated from all three sources are considered to have relatively more validity than results that emerge from one or two.

On each dimension of student outcomes, we used at least three kinds of measurement, employing qualitative and quantitative strategies, developmental frameworks, and recognition and production tasks. To study performance, we used academic reports of student progress in the curriculum, an external assessment in which students demonstrated their abilities in a half-day assessment session, and an integrated evaluation based on faculty ratings of how students demonstrated their abilities. Our study of perceptions included a perspectives interview, a survey of attitudes, and a questionnaire on career expectations and goals. We studied the human potential of our students from three separate theoretical frameworks: theories of cognitive development (Kohlberg, 1981; Loevinger, 1976; Perry, 1970; Mentkowski and others, 1983; Piaget, 1972; Rest, 1979), experiential learning theory and learning styles theory (Kolb, 1983), and measures of generic abilities, where the abilities are expected to link education and work performance (Watson and Glaser, 1964; Winter and others, 1981).

We also studied abilities across multiple points in time. We created a picture of student outcomes that resulted in a time series design: Students' emerging abilities were measured at the beginning, midpoint, and end of college. Thus, we created a cross sectional and longitudinal data base, conducting sets of parallel studies.

Our design involved collecting data from three major groups: our own students, our alumnae, and professionals who were not our alumnae. For this reason, we selected instrumentation that would enable us to compare findings from at least three kinds of measures. The student measures have already been described. We used a perspectives interview to study alumnae perceptions and a questionnaire to study their career development.

This year's alumnae studies will add independent measures of performance. Professionals' perceptions were studied through ratings of abilities critical for education, selection, and performance. Professionals' career development was measured through a questionnaire. A behavioral event interview tapped critical incidents of effective and ineffective professional performance. Most of these measures were created or drawn from job competence assessment techniques (McClelland, 1978; Klemp, 1978).

Finally, we studied abilities such that we had multiple opportunities for critique and comparison. Results generated through research and evaluation are compared first with data drawn from the curriculum; these data include the results of individual assessments and students' performance in course work. Second, research and evaluation results include student performance on standardized tests; this means that Alverno's results can be compared with the results obtained at other colleges. Third, the findings of research and evaluation studies are checked for consistency with the findings of similar research conducted elsewhere.

In sum, the four levels in our triangulated evaluation model represent our attempt to ensure that results emerge from multiplicity in measurement and theoretical frameworks. Since the college is conducting its own research and evaluation, it is critical that we build an external check into every level of the model. Multiplicity in measurement ensures breadth in qualitative and quantitative assessment; multiplicity in theoretical frameworks controls for bias in perspective and allows us to compare the faculty's own theories of learning and assessment with those drawn from outside the college. Performance and perceptions are measured with instruments designed at Alverno; measures of potential are drawn from outside the college. The professionals whom we used to evaluate particular abilities were drawn from groups of individuals who were not Alverno students or alumnae. Research and evaluation outcomes are compared with outcomes within the Alverno curriculum, but they are also compared with outside sources. Thus, multiple external opportunities for critique and comparison are built into each level of the triangulated model.

Characteristics of Evaluation. Frameworks and measures for validating outcomes needed to match the goals and assessment theory of the Alverno faculty as closely as possible. The instruments that we chose or created for each level of the model were derived from particular curriculum objectives and from principles of assessment design identified by the faculty. If we are adequately to validate student outcomes, our evaluation instruments must reflect the general characteristics of the faculty's techniques for assessing student performance. We must resist the temptation to adopt ready-made instruments as validation tools. For us, the faculty's definition of competence as developmental, holistic, and generic and the principles of assessment are our touchstones when we choose and create evaluation instruments.

A major task in applying the model was thus to select a battery of external criterion measures. We have not in practice been able to identify external criterion measures that perfectly match the abilities we are attempting to measure. We require each instrument that we use to include actual production tasks so that we can measure the learner in action. Our instruments must measure development over time and generate both qualitative and quantitative results. Finally, they must supply results that can be transformed into meaningful feedback for students (Messick, 1980). Few existing measures meet all these requirements.

Collegewide testing programs have been criticized for failing to relate the measured outcomes to later professional performance or to the personal growth outcomes expected of the liberal arts. Grade point averages and test scores appear to bear little relation to later success, and many measures of college outcomes have consequently come under fire as measuring knowledge without performance (McClelland, 1973). As a result, we used a variety of new approaches to measurement: They include measures of life span development, learning styles, and broad ability measures. We also used performance interviews and inventories of professionals as well as in-depth interviews of students and alumnae. At the same time, we used some traditional measures, such as the Critical Thinking Appraisal (Watson and Glaser, 1964) and standardized subject area tests, as a check on the results obtained with newer assessment techniques. We found that the newer methods take more time and involvement but that they are more efficient for other reasons. The descriptions of outcomes that these newer measures yield stimulate more discussion by faculty, and they seem to have more validity for performance after college. For example, by identifying the competences that make for effective performance in the nursing profession, we can build better in-college testing techniques and at the same time help to make existing state board examinations in nursing more performance based.

One advantage of using traditional criterion measures is that they allow us to compare our results with those obtained at other colleges. As members of a multi-institution consortium, we cooperated with McBer and Company, which administered several instruments at a range of colleges and universities with both highly selective and more open admission practices than our own (Winter and others, 1981). Rest (1979) maintains a clearinghouse on Defining Issues Test data, and Loevinger (1976) has some college student data on the Sentence Completion Test. These data have been useful for our comparisons of Alverno students with students at other colleges. Comparative data for the Perry scheme (Mines, 1982) and for Kohlberg's stages of moral development are also available (Kohlberg, 1981).

Faculty involvement is critical to the identification of research questions, to the execution of the studies, and to the critique and implementation of results (Rossi, 1982; Weiss, 1983). Ethical and effective student participation strategies are also vital; the strategies we have used have resulted in participation rates ranging from 83 to 99 percent. Several faculty groups have been essential to the entire evaluation effort. The Assessment Committee played a major role in designing and validating particular assessment techniques. Faculty have been able to create complex new instruments and apply them with the help of our own measurement and assessment professionals. Thus, our experience shows that faculty can, with professional help, do much of the work involved in creating cross-disciplinary production measures of abilities and that they also can judge student performance.

Furthermore, all faculty members have been actively involved in planning and carrying out strategies for involving students in the evaluation process. The dean's office and the Assessment Center collaborated to plan the administration of measures. Several departments collaborated with the Office of Research and Evaluation to conduct studies of professional perception and performance and used their credibility and contacts in the community to establish relationships with individuals and organizations. Several other offices in the college, including the Office of Career Development, the Office of Off-Campus Experiential Learning, the Development Office, and the President's Office, also became involved.

Benefits of Evaluation. Most evaluation is aimed at answering the question, Is the program working the way you claim it is? But, questions of quality assurance and program monitoring are not enough to fuel broad commitment to program evaluation, particularly since most of the information needed to answer them is readily available through the grapevine at a small college. Rather, the major impact of our research lies in the understanding that it has generated of the abilities that we are teaching for and of the ways in which students learn and develop them. We have found that, through research and evaluation, we have become better able to define and explore concepts like learning to learn, lifelong learning, and using-knowledge. Further, we are better able to describe individual differences in developmental patterns that can help us to individualize instruction. The insights that we have gained into student development and learning processes are not to be overlooked. They can give interdisciplinary discourse the power to cross barriers erected by the most independent department.

Ongoing intrainstitutional evaluation has raised the quality of other types of internal evaluation. Faculty outside the behavioral sciences are more willing to consider evaluation as part of curriculum development, because they no longer bear all the responsibility for a task whose roots are primarily outside their field. Expert staff are available to assist faculty with grants that call for explicit evaluation, and as a result faculty are more willing to enter into relationships with outside funding sources. Funding agencies are more likely to provide funds for a project that has the mind-set and demonstrated expertise for rigorous evaluation.

Evaluation efforts also directly benefit faculty by making it possible for them to improve instruction. Most educators, under the day-to-day pressure of classroom instruction, are open to identifying problems in teaching and to looking for solutions. When results from a cross-college effort are available on a continuing basis, excitement and discussion are common (Loacker, 1981). An effort like Alverno's enables faculty to measure things they really want to change; they are not restricted to measuring outcomes for which they are held accountable but that are not their own goals.

The opportunity that Alverno gives students to assess their own abilities helps them to structure their own vision of the learning process. It gives them a framework establishing the relevance of liberal education to their career, and it helps them to organize their professional development after college. Finding that abilities and processes transfer to their personal life during college frees them to become more open to areas of learning that do not directly relate to a specific occupation. The effort to identify and assess outcomes gives students an important experiential sense of their own competence that seems to be a major catalyst in their development in school and at work after college.

Students also benefit because they begin to feel that education is a process. Changes can and do occur, and students have input into program design and execution. A model like Alverno's allows students to view themselves as change agents within the institution, and it suggests a creative tension between the ideal and real while students are still in college. While alerting them to the imperfect role of authority, it prepares them for the dynamic interplay between their own expectations for change and the conditions that are necessary for making changes.

What Have We Learned?

We have learned that faculty can design and refine an ongoing assessment process. The fact that faculty continue to use, refine, and expand the assessment process with increasing expertise and enthusiasm provides primary testimony to its worth. Their continued interest rests on the results that they see in the development of their students. That interest is further supported by their own creative satisfaction and by the potential for research and publication that the assessment process consistently yields.

We have learned that a college can accomplish its own evaluation and validation. During the past decade, responding to demands for accountability usually meant contracting with an outside evaluation consultant or agency, which then developed and executed a design. Resources for such external evaluations are dwindling, and the persons who do such research are absent when the real work of evaluation—implementing the results—begins. Alverno built its own internal and external evaluation and validation mechanisms, and the resources channeled into validation served as seed money to develop the abilities of college faculty and staff. Now, consistent evaluation and validation studies are constantly under way, and they are supported by the college.

Finally, we have learned that research and evaluation efforts have benefits that extend beyond the particular institution or curriculum. Evaluation efforts in higher education also contribute to the educational research and evaluation community. Program evaluation is a new discipline, and it is being called on to provide technical assistance in the design of studies in a wide variety of field settings. New technologies must be created to meet the demand. Methods that work in some educational research settings are not necessarily transferable to the cross-disciplinary context of a liberal arts college or to more technologically oriented universities, where each discipline has its own well-developed methodologies. Efforts like Alverno's can provide guidelines for developing such techniques in new and different settings.

References

Alverno College Faculty. *Liberal Learning at Alverno College*. Milwaukee, Wisc.: Alverno Productions, 1976.

Alverno College Faculty. *Assessment at Alverno College*. Milwaukee, Wisc.: Alverno Productions, 1979.

Early, M., Mentkowski, M., and Schafer, J. *Valuing at Alverno: The Valuing Process in Liberal Education*. Milwaukee, Wisc.: Alverno Productions, 1980.

Klemp, G., Jr. *Job Competence Assessment*. Boston: McBer and Company, 1978.

Kohlberg, L. *The Meaning and Measurement of Moral Development*. Worcester, Mass.: Clark University Press, 1981.

Kolb, D. *Experiential Learning: Experience as the Source of Learning and Development*. Englewood Cliffs, N.J.: Prentice-Hall, 1983.

Loacker, G. "Revitalizing the Academic Disciplines by Clarifying Outcomes." In G. Loacker and E. G. Palola (Eds.), *Clarifying Learning Outcomes in the Liberal Arts*. New Directions for Experiential Learning, no. 12. San Francisco: Jossey-Bass, 1981.

Loacker, G., Cromwell, L., Fey, J., and Rutherford, D. *Analysis and Communication at Alverno College: An Approach to Critical Thinking*. Milwaukee, Wisc.: Alverno Productions, 1984.

Loevinger, J. *Ego Development: Conceptions and Theories*. San Francisco: Jossey-Bass, 1976.

McClelland, D. "Testing for Competence Rather Than for 'Intelligence.'" *American Psychologist*, 1973, *28*, 1-14.

McClelland, D. *Behavioral Event Interview*. Boston: McBer and Company, 1978.

Mentkowski, M., and Doherty, A. *Careering After College: Establishing the Validity of Abilities Learned in College for Later Careering and Professional Performance; Final Report to the National Institute of Education*. Milwaukee, Wisc.: Alverno Productions, 1983. (ED 239 556-239 566)

Mentkowski, M., and Doherty, A. "Abilities That Last a Lifetime." *American Association for Higher Education Bulletin*, 1984, *36* (6), 5-14.

Mentkowski, M., Moeser, M., and Strait, M. "Using the Perry Scheme of Intellectual and Ethical Development as a College Outcomes Measure: A Process and Criteria for Judging Student Performance." Paper presented at the annual meeting of the American Educational Research Association, Montreal, April 1983.

Messick, S. "Test Validity and the Ethics of Assessment." *American Psychologist,* 1980, *35,* 1012–1027.

Mines, R. "Student Development Assessment Techniques." In G. R. Hanson (Ed.), *Measuring Student Development.* New Directions for Student Services, no. 20. San Francisco: Jossey-Bass, 1982.

Perry, W., Jr. *Forms of Intellectual and Ethical Development in the College Years: A Scheme.* New York: Holt, Rinehart and Winston, 1970.

Piaget, J. "Intellectual Development from Adolescence to Adulthood." *Human Development,* 1972, *15,* 1–12.

Popham, W. *Criterion-Referenced Measurement.* Englewood Cliffs, N.J.: Prentice-Hall, 1978.

Rest, J. *Development in Judging Moral Issues.* Minneapolis: University of Minnesota Press, 1979.

Rossi, P. (Ed.). *Standards for Evaluation Practice.* New Directions for Program Evaluation, no. 15. San Francisco: Jossey-Bass, 1982.

Watson, G., and Glaser, E. *Critical Thinking Appraisal.* New York: Harcourt Brace Jovanovich, 1964.

Weiss, C. "The Stakeholder Approach to Evaluation: Origins and Promise." In A. S. Bryk (Ed.), *Stakeholder-Based Evaluation.* New Directions for Program Evaluation, no. 17. San Francisco: Jossey-Bass, 1983.

Winter, D., McClelland, D., and Stewart, A. *A New Case for the Liberal Arts: Assessing Institutional Goals and Student Development.* San Francisco: Jossey-Bass, 1981.

Marcia Mentkowski is director of the Office of Research and Evaluation and Professor of Psychology at Alverno College. She initiated and directs the college's research studies and works with her faculty colleagues to implement findings for instruction and assessment.

Georgine Loacker is professor of English at Alverno College. She serves as chairperson of the college's Assessment Committee, and she has written and conducted research on the process of individual assessment.

Constructing a longitudinal student outcomes data file takes careful planning and attention to detail, but investment in such a resource yields substantial dividends in the ability to document and explain complex patterns of student success.

Developing and Using a Longitudinal Student Outcomes Data File: The University of Colorado Experience

Jean Endo
Terry Bittner

Longitudinal student outcomes data files contain data on students that are collected by following specific cohorts of students over time. Such files are important for research on changes in student behaviors, attitudes, and abilities and for assessment of the impact of the college experience or specific institutional programs on student outcomes. Longitudinal data files are also necessary for research that involves tracking students' enrollment, academic progress, or both as they move term by term from freshman year to senior year. Studies that use such data files are becoming especially significant as a result of the need for institutions to be accountable to external constituencies, such as governing boards and state legislatures.

This chapter describes the development and use of a longitudinal student outcomes data file by the Office of Academic Planning at the

P. T. Ewell (Ed.). *Assessing Educational Outcomes.* New Directions
for Institutional Research, no. 47. San Francisco: Jossey-Bass, September 1985.

University of Colorado at Boulder. The university is a doctorate-granting research institution with approximately 21,000 students. Many of the details concerning the data file are specific to the university because of its particular programs, students, resources, and needs; they are not covered here. Nevertheless, the chapter will provide detail about the university's experience sufficient to provide the reader with insights into the development and use of such a file. Thus, this chapter covers four issues: designing the university's data file, building the university's data file, conducting studies to investigate issues, and presenting information to the university community. It concludes with recommendations based on the university's experience.

The University of Colorado first began to develop and use longitudinal student data files in 1975. Data have been collected over a ten-year period. Two freshman cohorts (1975 and 1981) have been followed over time. Since it has been important for the university to evaluate the educational experiences of its undergraduates and the effectiveness of its academic and support programs in a value-added manner, these files have always had a student outcomes focus. In recent years, the university has emphasized the recruitment of high-ability out-of-state students because of a state-mandated enrollment ceiling on in-state students and a projected national decline in the number of high school produce information necessary for enrollment management policies. To simplify the discussion, this chapter restricts its attention to the development and use of the 1981 cohort data file.

Designing the Longitudinal Student Outcomes Data File

Selecting the Variables. The variables to be included in the 1981 data file were selected by using university administrators, university staff, past studies and reports by various university offices, and research literature. Top university administrators were interviewed to define high-priority student-related issues that student data could address. During these interviews, it was important to discover why certain considered. For example, attrition was seen as a major issue because of its obvious impact on enrollments, and two of the many policy alternatives were the creation of new retention programs and the use of different tuition rates. The interview process established five priority issues: the confirmation rates of accepted university applicants and the size of the applicant pool, the attrition of currently enrolled students, the evaluation of residential academic programs, the assessment of the educational experiences of undergraduates, and alumni satisfaction with the university. To obtain further details, academic and support staff who dealt with these priority issues on a daily basis were interviewed. These interviews with university administrators and staff were critical in identifying variables for the data file.

As the priority issues were being discussed, it was necessary to decide which student subgroups might receive special attention. For instance, out-of-state students were a significant part of the confirmation rate/applicant pool issue because of their substantial contribution to tuition and their higher-than-average attrition rates. Determination of these subgroups was necessary so that they could be properly identified in the data file. The subgroups also needed attention later, when data were collected, so that we could make sure that there were sufficient individual cases for data analysis.

After the interviews had been completed, a university wide search was made for existing studies, reports, and memoranda related to the five priority issues. For example, reports and tables on student attrition were found in the offices of deans, academic departments, and minority student programs. Like the interviews, these materials were used to identify variables for the data file.

During this search for internal university documents, the extensive literature on subjects related to the five priority issues was reviewed along with research on student subgroups, such as ethnic minorities. This literature review turned up hundreds of possible variables for the data file, and some strategy had to be devised to select a manageable number. In this instance, it was decided to make use of existing conceptual frameworks that we encountered in the literature. Conceptual frameworks can be used to help select variables, because they usually offer explanations for a particular phenomenon, such as attrition. These frameworks identify key variables, describe relationships between variables, and even suggest methods of data analysis. When there were contrasting frameworks in the literature, the choice among them was based on their appropriateness for the University of Colorado. These frameworks were also used later to guide research on the five priority issues.

Frameworks by Maguire and Lay (1981), Litten (1979), and Dembowski (1980) that examine the effects of various factors on college choice were used to select variables for the confirmation/applicant pool issue. Tinto's (1975) model, which shows that attrition is affected by the degree to which a student is integrated into an institution's academic and social systems, was used to select variables for the attrition and student outcomes issues. In addition, work by Pascarella and Terenzini (Pascarella, 1980; Pascarella and Terenzini, 1978, 1980; Terenzini and Pascarella, 1980), Feldman and Newcomb (1969), Lenning and others (1977), and Pace (1971) was used for the student outcomes issue. The frameworks of Tinto (1975), Pascarella and Terenzini (1980), Lacy (1978), and Gaff (1970) were used to select variables for the residential academic programs issue. Finally, the National Center for Higher Education Management Systems (NCHEMS) outcomes structure (Lenning and others, 1977) and the preceding work on student outcomes were used to select variables for the alumni issue.

All the variables selected for the 1981 data file were carefully checked to determine that they could be measured in ways that would provide useful information. In addition, it was necessary to make sure that certain variables were included so that direct comparisons could be made with national studies or surveys such as those of the Cooperative Institutional Research Program (Astin and others, 1979), the NCHEMS/College Board questionnaires (Ewell, 1983), and the American College Testing Program (1979) surveys. Figure 1 lists the types of variables selected for the data file.

Defining a Student Cohort. At this point it was decided that, given the university's informational needs, it would be best to gather data on the selected variables by following a student cohort over time. The freshman year would receive special attention because previous research at the university showed that freshmen were the largest proportion of dropouts. Furthermore, recruitment efforts at the university focused primarily on freshman applicants, and the students enrolled in residential academic programs were predominantly freshmen.

For the 1981 data file, the cohort was defined as the 3,337 freshmen who were new to the university in the fall 1981 term. The definition excluded new nondegree students who were likely to be enrolled for only a few terms or on an intermittent basis. New freshman transfer students were also excluded, because they had earned their credits at other institutions, and they would therefore have different first-year educational experiences and complete their freshman year sooner than the rest of the cohort. For similar reasons, new sophomore, junior, and senior transfer students were not added to the cohort in subsequent years. The decision to omit these groups was made easier by the fact that the numbers were small. The transfer students might have been added if their numbers were relatively large as they are at many other institutions. In that case, studies on such issues as cohort attrition or graduation rates could have been conducted by removing the transfer students.

Sources of Data. Data on the 1981 cohort on the variables just specified were collected over time from university computer data files and questionnaires. Like most institutions, the university uses computer data files in its daily operations. Admissions master files contain admissions-related data, including students' demographic characteristics (for example, sex, residency status, ethnicity, age, and marital status), college entrance test scores, high school grades, and admissions status at the university. Enrollment term files contain course-related data for each enrolled student, such as the number of credit hours taken, grade point average, final course grades, major, and graduation data.

These two sources provided data for the 1981 data file on students' background characteristics, such as sex, residency status, ethnicity, college entrance test scores, high school percentile rank, and citizenship status; variables needed to track students' academic status, such as credit hours taken and grade point average by term; variables needed to track students' enrollment status, determine dropout rates, and identify students who left

Figure 1. Sources of Data for the 1981 Student Flow Data File

ADMISSIONS MASTER FILES AND ENROLLMENT TERM FILES

o University computer data files that contain admissions and course-related data; the types of variables below were extracted for the 1981 data file.

BACKGROUND CHARACTERISTICS

ACADEMIC STATUS VARIABLES

ENROLLMENT STATUS VARIABLES

GRADUATION-RELATED VARIABLES

STUDENT SUBGROUP VARIABLES

FRESHMAN QUESTIONNAIRE

o Examines the background characteristics, academic and social skills, achievements, experiences, expectations, and goals of incoming U. of Colorado freshmen.

BACKGROUND CHARACTERISTICS

Socioeconomic status
Financial support
Ethnicity
Residency status
Religion
Size of hometown

ACADEMIC ABILITY

High school grade point average
Intellectual/cultural interests

ASPIRATIONS/EXPECTATIONS

Advanced degree aspirations
Certainty of major
Certainty of career choice
Importance of completing college
Financial/emotional support from parents

IMPORTANCE OF GOALS FOR ATTENDING COLLEGE

PERSONALITY

Assertiveness
Academic and social self-confidence

(Administered in August 1981 to all new freshmen who planned to enroll at the U. of Colorado in the fall 1981 term)

SURVEY OF COLLEGE CHOICE

o Assesses the needs, perceptions, and expectations of U. of Colorado applicants; determines the influence of various persons/recruitment efforts on applicants' college choice. Identifies competing institutions; and examines factors related to enrollment at the University.

IMPORTANCE OF VARIOUS FACTORS IN THE FINAL SELECTION OF A COLLEGE

Size   Cultural opportunity
Location   Social opportunity
Quality   Financial aid
Cost

IMAGE OF THE U. OF COLORADO AND OTHER INSTITUTIONS BEING CONSIDERED

Size   Cultural opportunity
Location   Social opportunity
Quality   Financial aid
Cost

FINANCIAL AID

Amount of aid received at the U. of Colorado
Amount of aid received from another institution
Source of financial aid
Cost of U. compared with other institutions being considered

PREFERENCE FOR THE U. OF COLORADO AND OTHER INSTITUTIONS BEING CONSIDERED

Applicants' preference for the U. of Colorado
Parents preference for the U. of Colorado

INFLUENCE OF FRIENDS/RELATIVES WHO ATTENDED THE U. OF COLORADO ON CONFIRMATION

VISITED THE U. OF COLORADO

DISTANCE FROM HOME OF THE COLLEGE SELECTED

SATISFACTION WITH VARIOUS ADMISSIONS PROCEDURES FOR PROCESSING APPLICATIONS

HOW INFORMATION FROM VARIOUS SOURCES AFFECTED APPLICANTS' INCLINATION TO ENROLL AT THE U. OF COLORADO OR NEXT CHOICE INSTITUTION

EFFECT OF RECRUITMENT PROGRAMS/ACTIVITIES AND PUBLICATIONS ON ADMISSIONS DECISIONS

PLANS TO TRANSFER TO ANOTHER INSTITUTION

(Administered in August 1981 to all freshmen applicants who were accepted by the U. of Colorado for the fall 1981 term)

EDUCATIONAL EXPERIENCE SURVEY

o Examines the U. of Colorado students' satisfaction with various educational and social experiences, relationships with members of the University community, and participation in extracurricular activities.

SELF-ASSESSMENT OF:

Communication skills
Quantitative skills
Being widely read
Critical thinking skills
Personal independence
Interpersonal skills
Foreign language skills
Knowledge of basic facts

USE OF CAMPUS SERVICES

SATISFACTION WITH:

Frequency and quality of peer, faculty, and staff interaction
Quality of education
Social/cultural environment
Intellectual environment
Progress toward life goals
Grades
Campus services

WHETHER EXPECTATIONS WERE MET

PARTICIPATION IN EXTRACURRICULAR ACTIVITIES

HELP DESIRED ON:

Academic matters
Personal/social matters
Career-related matters

EVALUATION OF ACADEMIC PROGRAM

STUDY HABITS

(Administered during the spring 1982 term to 1981 freshmen who completed the Freshman Questionnaire and who were still enrolled at the U. of Colorado)

Figure 1. Sources of Data for the 1981 Student Flow Data File
(continued)

EXITING STUDENTS SURVEY

o Examines students' reasons for leaving the U. of Colorado, unmet needs, and future plans.

REASONS FOR LEAVING

TIME OF DEPARTURE

UNMET NEEDS

FUTURE PLANS

IF TRANSFERRED TO ANOTHER INSTITUTION:

 Selectivity of new institution
 Perceived image of new institution

(Administered during the spring 1983 term to 1981 freshmen who completed the Freshman Questionnaire and the Educational Experience Survey and who left the U. of Colorado after one year)

GRADUATING STUDENTS SURVEY

o Examines the same areas as the Educational Experience Survey and also graduates' future plans and degree of progress on specific college goals.

SELF-ASSESSMENT OF:

 Communication skills
 Quantitative skills
 Being widely read
 Critical thinking skills
 Personal independence
 Interpersonal skills
 Foreign language skills
 Knowledge of basic facts

PRESENT AND FUTURE PLANS

 Degree aspirations
 Desired job characteristics
 Career and job prospects

USE OF CAMPUS SERVICES

SATISFACTION WITH:

 Frequency and quality of peer, faculty, and
   staff interaction
 Quality of education
 Social/cultural environment
 Intellectual environment
 Progress toward life goals
 Grades
 Campus services

WHETHER EXPECTATIONS WERE MET

PARTICIPATION IN EXTRACURRICULAR ACTIVITIES

EVALUATION OF ACADEMIC PROGRAM

EXTENT OF PROGRESS TOWARD SPECIFIC GOALS

(Will be administered during the spring 1985 term to all 1981 freshmen who completed the Freshman Questionnaire and who were still enrolled at the U. of Colorado)

ALUMNI SURVEY

o Examines the U. of Colorado graduates' careers, assessments of their educational experiences, support for the University, and future plans.

EMPLOYMENT INFORMATION

 Job title
 Salary
 Career potential

CAREER ASPIRATIONS

INTERESTS, ACTIVITIES, AND PERSONAL GOALS

FUTURE PLANS

EVALUATION OF ACADEMIC PROGRAMS AT THE U. OF COLORADO

INTEREST IN HELPING THE U. OF COLORADO

(Will be administered during the spring 1987 term to all 1981 freshmen who completed the Freshman Questionnaire and who graduated from the U. of Colorado) the university; graduation-related variables, when available, to determine graduation rates after four, five, and six years; and variables needed to identify important student subgroups, such as veterans and scholarship students. These data were considered to be accurate and to have been collected in an appropriately disaggregated fashion and at appropriate times. Their use in the 1981 data file eliminated the need for collecting this information through questionnaires.

Questionnaires were used to collect data on the remaining data file variables. Several commercially produced instruments were considered, including those of the Cooperative Institutional Research Program (Astin and others, 1979), the NCHEMS/College Board Student Outcomes Information Service (Ewell, 1983), and the American College Testing Program (1979) Evaluation Survey Service. These instruments were attractive because of the accompanying processing services and the availability of national-level comparison data. However, it was decided to design special questionnaires tailored to the issues and variables that were important for the university. This decision made it necessary to use existing university resources to develop and administer the surveys, build the data file, and conduct the needed research. Six questionnaires were eventually designed: a survey of college choice, a freshman questionnaire, an educational experience survey, an exiting students survey, a graduating students survey, and an alumni survey. The types of variables on which these questionnaires collected data are shown in Figure 1.

The process of designing the six questionnaires began by organizing all the variables on which data were needed into time periods beginning with the preenrollment period and progressing through the senior year and alumni periods. This process suggested that six questionnaires were needed. Some minor adjustments were made, primarily to group similar kinds of variables; then efforts were directed toward the construction of the individual questionnaires.

Each questionnaire was constructed by following basic principles; these principles are reviewed by various authors, including Dillman (1978). In addition, we examined some existing instruments. All questions took what was already known about the university and its students into account. For example, income response categories reflected the very wide range of students' family incomes, and financial questions made allowances for the much higher tuition paid by out-of-state students. Special attention was given to arranging questions in a logical and meaningful fashion.

A preliminary draft of each questionnaire and its accompanying cover letter was reviewed by appropriate university administrators and staff and then pretested on samples of students. The final draft was then typed and photomechanically reduced so that it could be printed in four three-and-one-half inch columns on a legal-sized page. Individual questionnaires were printed on colored paper and folded to create documents with four three-and-one-half by eight-and-one-half inch panels. This format made the questionnaires easy to read and to handle, and it minimized mailing costs.

Before the questionnaires were distributed, each questionnaire was given a unique identification number so that the data for each student could be linked. During questionnaire pretests, it was discovered that students were much less sensitive to use of this number than to use of their regular student identification number. The cover letters explained the need for a unique number and assured students of confidentiality.

Individual questionnaires were sent through the mail along with prepaid self-addressed return envelopes; the freshman questionnaire and the educational experience survey were sent through the university mail system to students living on campus. A follow-up mailing to nonrespondents was usually conducted two weeks after the first mailing. Other follow-up efforts were made to enhance the response rates of specific student subgroups. For instance, Hispanic counselors were asked on one occasion to make personal telephone calls to Hispanic nonrespondents. Care was always taken to use methods and personnel who were sensitive to the characteristics of particular student subgroups. Response rates for the six questionnaires varied between 45 and 65 percent.

Building the Data File

This section describes the building of the university's 1981 data file. As noted earlier, data from the university's admissions master files and enrollment term files were used in the data file. Admissions master files are constantly updated, and there is one record for each student who applies to the university. Enrollment term files are constantly updated, and there is one record for each student who attends the university. Students are identified on both types of files by their student identification numbers. Most data are entered directly onto these files through on-line terminals or mark-sense sheets and optical readers.

The responses from each student questionnaire were coded and keypunched onto punched cards. While punched cards are cumbersome, using them made it easy to detect and correct data entry errors. Once the keypunching process had been completed, the data were stored in computer files.

Because of its sophisticated file manipulation capabilities, the Informatics Mark IV programming language was used to build the 1981 data file. Mark IV has automatic features that make it easy to match two or more different files to create another file containing some or all the information from the original files, and it has a transaction-processing feature for updating files. Other programming languages, such as COBOL, PL/1, FORTRAN, or BASIC, could have been used, but they are less convenient.

Later data analyses used the Statistical Package for the Social Sciences (SPSS).

Special Concerns. Several major questions had to be addressed before the 1981 data file was built. The questions included whether to use enrollment term file data from the beginning or end of a term, whether to include summer enrollment term file data, whether to include all or only some variables on the questionnaires, how to accommodate changes in the way data were coded, and what configuration to use for the data file.

It was decided to use enrollment term file data from the end of a term, not from the beginning. End-of-term data provided the maximum amount of information for a given term, including final course grades and credit hours earned. Data from summer enrollment term files were included in the 1981 data file. A significant proportion of the 1981 freshman cohort students took courses or dropped out during the summer. Because the university graduates students during the summer, graduation data on some students would be missing if summer sessions were excluded. All variables on the questionnaires were included in the data file, since the procedures described earlier had identified each of these variables as important. This decision increased data-processing and storage costs.

The manner in which data are coded can change over time. This problem was obviated for the student questionnaires by using identical coding schemes for the same variables. For data from the enrollment term files, coding changes were easy to detect; they were handled by making one person responsible for the maintenance of the data file and by creating good documentation. The 1981 data file was configured as a fixed-length eighty-character file so that it could accommodate SPSS. There was one record for each student. Each record was 2,400 characters in length—the equivalent of thirty eighty-character punched card images. Each record was identified by the student's identification number. Certain parts of each record were reserved for specific kinds of data, such as data from the freshman questionnaire.

Constructing the Data File. The 1981 data file was constructed in the following manner: First, relevant data for new 1981 freshmen were extracted from the fall 1981 admissions master file and placed in the data file. Next, data from the survey of college choice and the freshman questionnaire were added to the data file. Third, selected data from enrollment term files were added to the data file at the end of each term, starting with fall 1981. Graduation data from enrollment term files will be added to the data file at the appropriate times. Finally, data from subsequent questionnaires were added as soon as they became available.

Each addition to the data file matches student identification numbers in the data file with the unique questionnaire identification numbers or the student identification numbers in the enrollment term files and extracts the appropriate data. These matching procedures make it possible to link data on the same student from several different sources. Such linkages are necessary in a student flow data file for many reasons. Without them, variables from two or more different sources cannot be examined in the same bivariate or multivariate analyses, and the investigation of changes on specific variables (for example, which students changed their behaviors or attitudes between two points in time and why?) is precluded.

After each addition was made to the data file, frequency distributions on all new variables were obtained in order to check for data entry errors that had been overlooked. A corrected version of the data file was then stored so that it could be easily retrieved.

Conducting Studies to Investigate Issues

The 1981 data file has often been used to provide information on issues of interest to university administrators and staff. Information was often generated because of questions or requests related to routine university operations or programmatic and policy planning. Some information was produced because of research planned during the file's design.

On many occasions, the data file was used to furnish only a few pieces of information. However, several major studies were also undertaken to investigate various issues comprehensively, and other, smaller studies were conducted on aspects of these issues. Each large or small study involved the four basic research steps outlined in this section. A 1984 study of attrition will be used to illustrate these steps.

Creating an Analysis Design. The creation of an analysis design involved four operations: defining the research questions to be answered, determining the relevant variables, locating data on these variables in the data file, and selecting methods of data analysis. In order to define research questions for the attrition study, it was helpful to review the original concerns of university administrators and staff and to reexamine existing university documents dealing with attrition. From this review and reexamination, it was clear that an attrition study had to address five questions: First, how many students leave the university? Second, what types of students drop out? Third, what do students do when they leave the university? Fourth, why do students leave the university? Fifth, what can the university do to reduce attrition? Another review of the literature on attrition helped to pinpoint relevant variables and useful methods of data analysis.

Examining Student Characteristics. The second step in conducting a study involves examining the characteristics of the students whose data would be analyzed. Possible biases needed to be identified if these students were not representative of those in the entire cohort. In the attrition study, students in the cohort were representative of all freshmen except in respect to residency status, major, and adademic ability. In this instance, adjustments were not made through weighting procedures, because there were few cases in some subgroups. A report on the study's findings included a warning about possible biases.

Analyzing the Data. The third step in conducting a study involves analyzing the data. While data analysis can often be done effectively by using simple procedures like cross-tabulations and bivariate measures of association, multivariate statistical techniques were preferred whenever the data and problem were appropriate. Multivariate techniques were especially necessary for investigating changes in students' characteristics over time and the impact of programs on student outcomes. In the attrition study, factor-analytic procedures were used to develop a number of measures. After controlling for students' background characteristics, much of the analysis made use of discriminant analysis techniques to concentrate on university environmental factors that might affect attrition.

To address the first research question, enrollment tracking data drawn from university data files were used to identify the number of 1981 freshmen who left the university after one and two years. These findings were compared with data from the 1975 freshman cohort and with data from several comparable public universities. To examine the second question, data from university data files were presented in univariate tables to describe the demographic characteristics of dropouts. The third research question was investigated with data from the exiting students survey displayed in univariate tables. The last two questions were addressed with data from university data files, the freshman questionnaire, and the educational experience survey. Discriminant analysis procedures were used to determine which environmental variables affected attrition after one year and to produce classification functions that could predict whether any new freshman students would drop out after one year. While the findings from the attrition study were too extensive to summarize here, it can be noted that academic ability, the helpfulness of faculty, and the personal nature of the university all seemed to affect attrition.

Interpreting the Findings and Developing Recommendations. The last step in conducting a study involves interpretation of findings and development of recommendations. The results of a study were usually interpreted in a broad manner that had practical implications for the university. Care was taken to distinguish strong from weak findings. Where possible, recommendations were derived from specific sets of results. The cost-effectiveness of alternative recommendations was considered. Early versions of a study's findings, interpretations, and recommendations were reviewed by university administrators and staff who were familar with the issue under analysis. In the attrition study, one interpretation of certain findings was that the quality of contacts with university faculty, staff, and peers affected attrition. Eleven recommendations were formulated. One recommendation was that programs to increase student-faculty interaction outside the classroom setting needed to be developed.

All studies conducted with the 1981 data file followed the four-step process just outlined. The studies that were conducted included research on confirmation decisions by accepted freshman applicants, evaluation of two residential academic programs, assessment of freshman year outcomes, and general investigations of university applicants, freshmen, graduating seniors, dropouts, and alumni.

Presenting Information to the University Community

Information from studies that used the 1981 data file was usually presented in reports. Each report began with a statement of the problem and with reasons why research into the problem was important for the university. When particular conceptual frameworks were used, they were described. If one or more types of questionnaires had been used to collect the data, the process was outlined. The background characteristics of the students whose data were being analyzed were described, and the possible biasing effects of those characteristics were noted.

Analysis of the data was described in a logical fashion; often it followed a developmental or chronological order. If numerous analyses had to be presented, the major analyses were usually described in detail, and the others were summarized; the discussions were divided into sections and subsections. Analyses for the entire cohort were presented before analyses for student subgroups, unless subgroups were the primary objects of attention.

Complex statistical analyses were described in a straightforward and simple manner. Often they were supplemented with bivariate tables. For instance, after explaining that in a multiple regression analysis variable A had an effect on variable B, the report often included a bivariate table with percentages. Special efforts were taken to make tables easy to read.

Recommendations were presented at the end of the reports. The most cost-effective recommendations were given first. They were followed, first, by those that would have the greatest impact, then by those that could be tried if there were additional resources and by those that would have lesser impacts. Since recommendations often received more attention than the rest of a report, they were written with great care. Each report included a one-page executive summary describing the major findings, interpretations, and recommendations. The summary allowed busy individuals to review the study quickly and decide whether and when to read the entire report. Reports were usually distributed to university administrators and staff who could (and often did) implement the recommendations. Any subsequent distribution was generally made by their offices.

Data in the 1981 data file were sometimes analyzed to provide only a few pieces of information. The resulting information was most often presented orally or through memoranda. Recent examples include information on the attrition rates of freshmen in residential academic programs (for the chancellor and the board of regents), student outcomes after one year (for the state auditor's office and the Office of State Planning and Budgets), future plans and expectations of the 1981 freshmen (for the university president), and career interests of freshman psychology majors (for the psychology department).

Ten Recommendations

It is clear from the University of Colorado's experience that longitudinal student outcomes data files are invaluable for research on marketing, attrition, program evaluation, and other outcomes. This experience highlights several broad lessons for other institutions that would like to build and use such files:

1. A longitudinal data file should be carefully designed. Major issues and variables should be identified in consultation with institutional administrators and staff and through an examination of existing documents. A review of the relevant literature is important for suggesting appropriate variables, conceptual frameworks, and data analysis procedures.

2. The greatest possible use should be made of data from existing institutional records, such as enrollment files. Questionnaires should be used to fill critical informational gaps.

3. Available instruments and references on question writing and questionnaire construction, such as Dillman (1978) should be consulted when questionnaires are created.

4. If such resources as time, money, or research expertise are limited, an institution should consider using only data from institutional records or perhaps these data together with data from one or two short questionnaires. The use of commercially produced instruments is another alternative. In addition, the drain on resources can be minimized by gathering data on a sample of a given student cohort. However, sample attrition owing either to nonresponse or to actual attrition must be taken into account so that there will be sufficient data and no important sample biases.

5. A student flow data file should be maintained so that it can furnish information in response to questions or requests from institutional administrators and staff as well as data for planned research.

6. When research is conducted, multivariate statistical techniques are preferable if they are appropriate for the problem and data. Research on changes in student behaviors, attitudes, and abilities or the impact of college or specific institutional programs on student outcomes presents special problems, which must be addressed (see, for example, Harris, 1962; Feldman, 1972; Astin, 1970a, 1970b).

7. The results of a study should be presented in a relatively simple, straightforward manner. Furthermore, feedback should be obtained from institutional administrators and staff on early versions of the study's findings and recommendations.

8. The identity of individual students must be kept confidential when data are collected, stored, analyzed, and reported. Students should be identified on questionnaires and in data files only by numbers. After questionnaires are processed, they should be stored securely. Access to the data file should be limited to authorized individuals.

9. Development of a longitudinal data file is time-consuming and costly the first time it is done, but subsequent cycles should require fewer resources. However, it should be expected that the data file will be revised so that new institutional issues can be investigated. Obviously, the nature and timing of new cycles depend on specific institutional characteristics and the availability of resources.

10. Finally, the development and use of a longitudinal data file should be seen as a significant undertaking. Consequently, it is important to plan ahead, to have adequate resources, to anticipate future problems, and—especially—to allow much more time than initially seems to be necessary.

References

American College Testing Program. *The ACT Evaluation Survey Service Users' Guide.* Iowa City, Iowa: American College Testing Program, 1979.

Astin, A. W. "The Methodology of Research on College Impact, Part One." *Sociology of Education,* 1970a, *43* (3), 223–254.

Astin, A. W. "The Methodology of Research on College Impact, Part Two." *Sociology of Education,* 1970b, *43* (4), 437–450.

Astin, A. W., King, M. R., and Richardson, G. T. *The American Freshman: National Norms for Fall 1979.* Los Angeles: Cooperative Institutional Research Program and American Council on Education, 1979.

Dembowski, F. L. "A Model for Predicting Student College Choice." *College and University,* 1980, *55* (2), 103–112.

Dillman, D. A. *Mail and Telephone Surveys.* New York: Wiley, 1978.

Ewell, P. T. *Student Outcomes Questionnaires: An Implementation Handbook.* Boulder, Colo.: National Center for Higher Education Management Systems and the College Board, 1983.

Feldman, K. A. "Difficulties in Measuring and Interpreting Change and Stability During College." In K. A. Feldman (Ed.), *College and Student.* New York: Pergamon Press, 1972.

Feldman, K. A., and Newcomb, T. M. *The Impact of College on Students.* Vol. 1: *An Analysis of Four Decades of Research.* San Francisco: Jossey-Bass, 1969.

Gaff, J. G. and Associates. *The Cluster College.* San Francisco: Jossey-Bass, 1970.

Harris, C. W. (Ed.). *Problems in Measuring Change.* Madison: University of Wisconsin Press, 1962.

Lacy, W. B. "Interpersonal Relationships as Mediators of Structural Effects: College

Student Socialization in a Traditional and an Experimental University Environment." *Sociology of Education*, 1978, *51* (4), 210–211.

Lenning, O. T., Lee, Y. S., Micek, S. S., and Service, A. L. *A Structure for the Outcomes of Postsecondary Education*. Boulder, Colo.: National Center for Higher Education Management Systems, 1977.

Litten, L. H. "Market Structure and Institutional Position in Geographic Market Segments." *Research in Higher Education*, 1979, *11* (1), 59–83.

Maguire, J. J., and Lay, R. "Modeling the College Choice Process: Image and Decision." *College and University*, 1981, *56* (2), 123–139.

Pace, C. R. *Higher Education Measurement and Evaluation KIT*. Los Angeles: Center for Study and Evaluation, Graduate School of Education, University of California, 1971.

Pascarella, E. T. "Student-Faculty Informal Contact and College Outcomes." *Review of Educational Research*, 1980, *50* (4), 545–595.

Pascarella, E. T., and Terenzini, P. T. "Student-Faculty Informal Relationships and Freshman-Year Educational Outcome." *Journal of Educational Research*, 1978, *71* (4), 183–189.

Pascarella, E. T., and Terenzini, P. T. "Student-Faculty and Student-Peer Relationships as Mediators of the Structural Effects of Undergrauate Residence Arrangement." *Journal of Educational Research*, 1980, *73* (6), 344–353.

Terenzini, P. T., and Pascarella, E. T. "Student-Faculty Relationships and Freshman-Year Educational Outcomes: A Further Investigation." *Journal of College Student Personnel*, 1980, *21* (6), 521–528.

Tinto, V. "Dropout from Higher Education: A Theoretical Synthesis of Recent Research." *Review of Educational Research*, 1975, *45* (1), 89–125.

Jean Endo is assistant director of the Office of Academic Planning at the University of Colorado at Boulder. She has developed student outcomes data files at the university and conducted research on marketing, attrition, student outcomes, and alumni.

Terry Bittner was a systems analyst at the University of Colorado at Boulder for ten years, where he was instrumental in developing an office automation system that networked microcomputers at the university. After receiving his M.B.A. degree, he started his own computer consulting business, which specializes in office automation systems and software development.

*Follow-up studies of former students provide
information on the bottom line for institutions of
higher education. Careful planning, early involvement
of users of the information, and multiple data
presentation strategies are some keys to success for such
studies.*

Designing Follow-Up Studies of Graduates and Former Students

*Mike Stevenson, R. Dan Walleri
Saundra M. Japely*

Student follow-up results provide one form of outcomes measurement that can be used to address issues of accountability, program review, community relations, and marketing. Although follow-up results are an almost ideal measure for demonstrating accountability, they are underutilized for this purpose. How satisfied are students with the educational services they receive, especially after they have some time in which to reflect? What value do former students think their education has had to further subsequent career experiences? Follow-up studies provide a bottom line for institutions of higher education.

This chapter discusses the practical mechanics of conducting student follow-up surveys. Each step of the process is discussed: definition of purpose, constituency support, survey design, questionnaire design, administration procedures, analysis, and presentation of results. Points are illustrated by practice at Mt. Hood Community College (MHCC), a medium-sized, suburban comprehensive community college located near Portland, Oregon.

P. T. Ewell (Ed.). *Assessing Educational Outcomes.* New Directions
for Institutional Research, no. 47. San Francisco: Jossey-Bass, September 1985.

Defining the Purposes of the Study

Establishing the purposes of a student follow-up survey helps to determine the survey population, questionnaire content, and frequency of follow-up. Purposes can be defined by identifying who is to use the results and how the results will be used to serve specific external and institutional needs.

External Factors. Accreditation and government reporting requirements are a major external impetus for student follow-up studies. For example, the federal Vocational Education Act requires student follow-up for community college vocational programs; the requirement is aimed at determining the degree to which students secure program-related jobs (Datta, 1979). State coordinating boards are also often involved with student follow-up. In Oregon, efforts are currently under way to integrate federal, state, and accreditation needs for student follow-up so as to reduce duplication of effort and maximize the usefulness of follow-up results. At the state level, student follow-up results can prove beneficial by informing state boards, commissions, and legislatures about the return on state support for higher education (Friedlander, 1982).

Normally, external requirements only define minimum standards for student follow-up. The actual scope and utility of such studies for a particular institution will vary with management style, information needs, and the level of resources that can be dedicated to the effort.

Internal Factors. Outcomes research is often viewed in negative terms. The assumption is that its only purpose is to identify institutional or program weaknesses. However, follow-up results can also be used in a positive fashion, for example in program review and improvement, in efforts to improve community relations, and in efforts to develop effective marketing. Although follow-up results are only one of several elements used in program review, they constitute one of the better sources of evidence on program effectiveness. Community relations are especially important for colleges that rely on local tax support; many community colleges and four-year institutions with a strong urban or regional identity fall into this category. Positive follow-up results can enhance such support. Marketing has become increasingly important as much of higher education has experienced retrenchment. Marketing efforts can be considerably enhanced by follow-up results that document the successes of former students.

However, if follow-up studies are to have an impact within the institution, their results must be integrated with the institution's planning, review, and budgeting processes. Otherwise, follow-up reports are likely to gather dust, rather than inform critical decisions affecting the future of programs. Defining the purposes of student follow-up surveys from the outset allows an institution to establish an appropriate role for follow-up results within its decision-making process.

Soliciting Support and Involvement

Once the purposes for a student follow-up survey have been established, the support and involvement of interested parties throughout the institution should be encouraged. This involvement will not only shape the design of the survey; it will also increase the prospects that the results will be used. If there are federal or state reporting requirements, some form of statewide coordination and standardization will also be required. In Oregon, coordination is provided by the State Department of Education through an advisory committee composed of representatives from the state's community colleges. At the institutional level, administrators, faculty, students, and advisory committee members should be consulted. The involvement of campus groups can be extended to include help in conducting the survey itself. At MHCC, faculty sign the cover letter sent to their program's former students. This practice has helped to increase the response rate, and it has increased faculty identification with the research process.

Three years ago, MHCC formed a student success task force that included students, faculty, and staff. This group wrestled with the problem of defining student success and explored new college policies and procedures that might improve students' prospects of achieving their objectives at the college. These efforts resulted in a major addition to MHCC's student follow-up process: the collection of data about student intentions and analysis relating outcomes to expressed intentions.

Designing the Structure of the Survey

An important step of the process is to design the survey itself. Some elements of the design may be set by state boards or departments so that results can be used to prepare statewide summary reports. For example, in Oregon all vocational graduates and nonreturning full-time students from the previous fall term must be surveyed within six to nine months after the end of each academic year. At MHCC, all graduates (vocational and lower-division transfer students) and all nonreturning students who were full-time in any term of the previous academic year are surveyed. This practice increases the survey population by about one-third and provides a more representative sample of the total student population.

Survey Population. Determining which students to survey and when to survey them is a key issue, which is complicated by institutional type and cost considerations. Surveying all graduates and nonreturning students for a given year each year or every few years is a fairly straightforward approach. Sampling is another approach, but it has important limitations. At MHCC, the cost of surveying almost 20,000 students a year is prohibitive, and only full-time students are surveyed. If an institution has a computer-based student tracking system, the follow-up survey can be integrated with or linked to this system. A computer-based system assists in determining the survey population and allows the characteristics of survey respondents and nonrespondents to be compared.

Institutions with a large part-time student population have special problems in conducting follow-up studies, especially as regards cost. As already noted, MHCC focuses on full-time students. MHCC follow-up results have to be qualified as a result, since half of the total student population consists of part-time students.

Survey Timing. At MHCC, follow-up questionnaires are mailed to graduates and former students approximately nine months after they leave the institution. This time frame gives them ample time in which to make some value judgments about their educational experiences, to secure employment in a field related to their education, or to continue their education at another institution.

Program-Level Results. A critical issue in determining the survey population is whether results are needed for individual programs. Where such results are important, sampling is seldom an appropriate approach, since the number surveyed for any given program is generally too small to yield statistically significant results. Individual programs are the decision focus for most administrators and faculty; thus, the value of student follow-up surveys is likely to be determined by the distribution of response rates across programs. While common practice in community colleges indicates that surveys obtain response rates of between 40 and 60 percent, these rates vary greatly by program. Some programs at MHCC traditionally have high response (for example, nursing), while others are consistently low. Since administrators and faculty may tend to discount results based on a small absolute number of respondents, it is important to emphasize the total surveyed for a given program. For example, if there are four respondents, the response may appear to be low, but if there were only six graduates of the program, the response rate is relatively good, and the results are relatively sound.

Designing or Choosing the Survey Instrument

The key elements in any student follow-up survey are the content, type, and structure of the actual questions asked. There are basically two options: a self-designed instrument or the services provided by such organizations such as the American College Testing (ACT) program, the National Center for Higher Education Management Systems, and the College Board. The advantage of external organizations is that they reduce the amount of time and effort that the individual institution has to commit to designing an adequate questionnaire. These organizations often provide data analysis services and comparative reports as well. At the same time, a self-designed instrument improves the fit between the questionnaire's content and the institution's concerns. It can also be less costly. At our institution, we use three different self-designed questionnaires: one for vocational students, one for lower-division transfer students, and one for GED/developmental education students. Flexibility in analysis and reporting is another advantage of self-design, especially when computer resources and software appropriate to these tasks are available.

Core Questions and Format. Self-designed or standardized, questionnaires usually address a common core of issues. Most follow-up questionnaires contain questions about the student's further education, occupational and career experiences, and the knowledge and skills gained at the institution and their relevance to the student's current situation. The questionnaire should be short (so that it takes between five and ten minutes to complete), clear, and professional in appearance (typeset if possible). Four pages should be enough. Remember to include a cover letter and space for comments. Long and complicated questionnaires should be avoided because they tend to reduce the response rate.

Program staff sometimes ask the instrument's developers to include certain items pertaining to specific concerns. Such requests can often be accommodated by means of a one-page insert. Space should not be wasted asking questions to which student records already provide the answers (for example, sex, race, student major, and grade point average).

Confidentiality. The cover letter must emphasize that individual responses will be kept confidential. (This is especially important at MHCC, where the cover letter is often signed by program instructors.) Situations may arise where administrators or faculty ask to know an individual student's identity, usually so they can follow up on a comment that the student has made. In such cases, survey staff should contact the student to secure his or her permission to release his or her identity. Confidentiality is a professional as well as a legal responsibility, and it should be so considered by survey staff.

Establishing Survey Procedures

Methods of Data Collection. Institutions use many methods to conduct follow-up surveys, including telephone surveys, mailed surveys, face-to-face interviews, and combinations of these three methods. The best method depends on the relative importance of several factors. Cost, questionnaire length and construction, the response rate desired, the accuracy of responses, and the ability to obtain a representative sample are just a few of the factors that need to be considered.

Each method of data collection has its strengths and weaknesses, as Figure 1 shows. Before choosing a particular method, those who are to conduct the survey should review the institution's priorities. If the institution places a high priority on keeping costs down and on obtaining a

Figure 1. Evaluating Methods of Data Collection

Criteria	Methods of Data Collection		
	Mail	Telephone	In-Person
Cost	Medium	Low	High
Allowable Complexity	Medium	Low	High
Obtaining Accurate Responses	High	Medium	Low
Response Rate	Low	Medium	High
Completeness	Medium	High	High
Potential for Bias	Low	High	High

Note: The ratings are only approximate and are relative to one another. This table is a summarized version of a table prepared by Larry Benedict, University of Massachusetts, Amherst as presented in *Using Student Information to Impact the College,* National Center for Higher Education Management Systems (NCHEMS), 1980.

high response rate, it is probably not advisable to administer a lengthy questionnaire by telephone. Interviewer bias can distort responses in face-to-face data collection situations. Therefore, if accuracy is a high priority, it may be desirable to choose another collection strategy or to monitor the behavior of interviewers carefully. If survey completeness is tantamount and the questionnaire contains open-ended questions, better responses can be solicited in person than by mail, where respondents may simply skip over such questions. Which method of data collection to use depends on which factors are important to the institution.

By far the most common technique used in student follow-up studies is the mailed survey. The relatively low cost and relatively high reliability of the data collected by this method make it a popular choice. Dillman (1978) outlines surveying procedures step by step.

Tracking Survey Responses. The efficiency of the survey process can be enhanced by preparing a logbook at the outset of a survey to track the status of individual responses. At MHCC, the logbook divides students by major code, and each student is assigned a unique identifying number. Logbook columns should be reserved for recording response status from the first mailing, from subsequent mailings, and from telephone contacts when needed. At MHCC, the student identification number and major code are placed on the face of the questionnaire before it is mailed. When a questionnaire is returned, it is easy to identify and match the respondent's identification number and to log the student's questionnaire as returned. This type of record-keeping system facilitates the survey process and allows for verification of the data if it is required at some later time.

Strategies for Maximizing Response Rate. A large proportion of the surveys that will be returned are returned within a few days after respondents receive the first mailing. To bolster response rate, the first mailing is followed by a second request to nonrespondents approximately three weeks later. The second request is essentially the same packet as the first; it includes a survey questionnaire and a self-addressed stamped return envelope. However, the cover letter is new. It makes a stronger request for response. The second mailing usually generates another flurry of responses.

As the third step, to alleviate concern about bias from early returns and to increase the response rate, student workers telephone those who still have not responded after another three weeks have passed. If contact is made, the survey is administered by telephone. This technique usually nets the last third of the responses received. Comments offered over the telephone are generally briefer and less thoughtful than those received by mail, but basic data about the student's activity since leaving the institution are collected, and they are valuable.

One institution, concerned about the presumed bias of early mailed returns, compared responses from students who returned the questionnaire directly after receiving it with responses from students who did not respond by mail but who agreed to answer the questionnaire in a short telephone interview. The researchers found that there was very little difference between the two groups of respondents (Quinley and others, 1983). Nonetheless, nonresponse can be a critical issue. Students can be a very mobile population, and survey response rates vary by institutional type and size. Any design technique that helps to increase the quantity and quality of survey responses should be explored. At MHCC, the registrar's office helps by including a one-page letter with each graduate's diploma requesting an up-to-data permanent address. The student-supplied addresses are much more reliable than the addresses in institutional records. At other institutions, records maintained by the alumni office may provide the most accurate current address.

At MHCC, program instructors sign the survey cover letter. This serves to personalize each request for information. The request comes not from an anonymous researcher but from an instructor with whom students are familiar. To further increase the chances of a good response rate, instructors sometimes help by supplying information on students' whereabouts— either addresses or places of employment.

Use of Direct Incentives. To increase survey response rates, some institutions have offered incentives in the form of money or store coupons. This small token of appreciation conveys the message that the researcher appreciates the effort involved in responding (Dillman, 1978).

MHCC experimented with the incentive concept during its 1978–79 follow-up survey. A notice was included in the first mailing of the questionnaire notifying students that a packet of coupons would be mailed to them when their response was received. Seven local firms participated in the coupon offer, including Kentucky Fried Chicken, McDonald's, Dunkin' Donuts, Wright's Jewelers, Dairy Queen, the College Bookstore, and the Aquatic Center. It is difficult to assess the full impact of the coupon incentive on the response rate. However, comparison with the response rates obtained in other years suggests that the coupon incentive slightly improved the overall response rate.

Data Compilation. After the questionnaires have been returned, the task of compiling the data begins. MHCC uses a fourth-generation computer language to create an easy-to-use data input screen. The screen references survey questions in the same order in which they appear on the survey instrument. Each response category is assigned a simple number code.

Workstudy, student aides, or part-time clerical help can be employed at a reasonable rate to do most of the labor required for data compilation. Depending on the size of the institution, one or two part-time workers should be able to keep track of respondent status, input raw data into the computer (or tally responses by hand), and type verbatim comments.

After all data have been entered, a different employee verifies the data entry by checking a 10 percent random sample for accuracy. If data entry errors are found, a more thorough check can be undertaken. Canned statistical packages, such as SPSS or SAS, can be used to perform additional data edit checks.

Verbatim Comments. Since the recording of verbatim comments is the most time-consuming task in data compilation, it is helpful to have them typed as soon as they arrive. At MHCC, a word processor is used to record comments on a floppy disk; additional responses can be inserted as they are received. Since some comments may be less than complimentary, workers must be made aware of the sensitive and confidential nature of the information with which they are working. Faculty names are usually not included in the comments, which are otherwise transcribed verbatim.

Analyzing and Presenting Results

The depth and the scope of the presentation of survey results depend both on the intended audience and on the use to which the data will be put. It is obvious that the board of education and instructors need very different selections of data. Faculty may be looking for information on how specific course offerings within a particular department or discipline can be improved, whereas board members are interested in more general data—trends in satisfaction levels or long-range projections of institutional effectiveness.

Regardless of the audience, statistical data are much easier to comprehend and digest when they are displayed graphically. Pie charts, bar graphs, or line graphs can all be used to complement the tables and narrative portions of a report. A microcomputer business graphics package can be purchased for this purpose at a reasonable cost. A mix of narrative, tables, and graphs generally serves to make the data easy to understand.

Types of Reports. At MHCC, a separate report is presented to the college's board of education. This report presents an overall view of the responses received from all students. It includes year-by-year trends, which can be helpful in relating follow-up results to the larger local context. For example, when the local economy is depressed, the number of students reporting difficulty in securing employment will undoubtedly increase regardless of program effectiveness.

Follow-up data reports are also submitted to the Oregon Department of Education, which prepares a statewide summary report on all the community colleges. In turn, this statewide report is sent to members of the legislature, to business groups, and to other organizations that take an interest in outcomes research.

One important use of follow-up data is as an aid to decision making in individual programs and curricula. At MHCC, there is a separate report for each discipline; the report is sent directly to the faculty and manager responsible for the given program. For example, faculty in the physical therapy program receive summary information and verbatim comments from students who were enrolled in the program, business management faculty receive information on business management students, and so on. The individual discipline reports give faculty and managers a way of reviewing and analyzing their own discrete programs, courses, and instructors.

Practical Uses of Follow-up Results. When follow-up results are used in concert with other information, a good picture of program effectiveness can be painted. Other information can include student demand data, program cost, retention rates, facilities costs, employment outlook, discipline and course enrollment, and student completion rate. Decisions regarding changes in program format or curriculum can be influenced by such information (Stevenson and Walleri, 1981). For example, as a result of program reviews at MHCC, the real estate, cosmetology, and floristry programs changed the emphasis of offerings from two-year associate degrees to the basic courses that students need to become employable. The supervision in business and industry faculty incorporated work life experiences into the program curriculum as a direct result of student comments on follow-up questionnaires. Many other curriculum changes have been made as a result of MHCC's program review process, a process in which student follow-up results play a critical role.

Student success stories gleaned from follow-up studies can be used as a community relations tool. Historically, institutions have measured their effectiveness by the number of degrees granted. This measure of success means little to the public at large. However, publicizing the achievements of former students that can be attributed to their educational experiences can generate a positive public response.

The Changing Nature of Student Follow-up

As MHCC has conducted cyclical student follow-up studies over the years, it has learned that the process of measuring student outcomes is not static. As the educational enterprise evolves and as the characteristics of the students served change, follow-up procedures must adapt accordingly (Dennison, 1983). Influenced by the California Longitudinal Study (Hunter and Sheldon, 1980), we recently recognized a major difficulty in correctly interpreting the student outcomes measured. For example, many vocational students leave the institution before graduating. Although these students can be viewed as dropouts, it may also be the case that the institution has misperceived their intent. If the student's primary intent is to get a job, then it is likely that he or she will forgo program completion and graduation if employment becomes an option. As a result, MHCC has initiated a survey of student intentions at the time of registration, and it updates these intentions in each subsequent term that the student enrolls. With these data, the institution can now evaluate student outcomes in the light of students' expressed intentions. As a result, graduation rates, student persistence, and student outcomes can be measured and explained with greater precision and sensitivity. The institution can respond to demands for accountability while controlling for questionable assumptions about students' objectives.

Conclusion

The primary criterion of success for student follow-up studies is the extent to which the information obtained from former students influences decisions that will benefit currently enrolled and future students. While those who conduct a student follow-up survey must keep many things in mind, they must always keep the eventual impact of the results in sight. Four points need to be underlined: Assessing the informational needs of specific campus user groups is the critical first step. Involving these user groups in planning the survey pays large dividends. The use of multiple follow-up strategies is superior to any single approach. Finally, presenting the results professionally in many ways—in writing, by means of graphs and comparisons, in formal oral presentations, and in informal discussions—is the essential and very rewarding last step.

References

Datta, L. "Better Luck This Time: From Federal Legislation to Practice in Evaluating Vocational Education." In T. Abramson, C. K. Tittle, and L. Cohen (Eds.), *Handbook of Vocational Education Evaluation.* Beverly Hills, Calif.: Sage, 1979.

Dennison, J. D. *A Longitudinal Follow-up Survey of Students from Career/Technical Programs in British Columbia Community Colleges and Institutions. Summary Report.* Vancouver, B.C., 1983. (ED 238 473).

Dillman, D. *Mail and Telephone Surveys: The Total Design Method.* New York: Wiley, 1978.

Friedlander, J. "ERIC Sources and Information: Measuring the Benefits of Community Colleges." In R. Alfred (Ed.), *Institutional Impacts on Campus, Community, and Business Constituencies.* New Directions for Community Colleges, no. 38. San Francisco: Jossey-Bass, 1982.

Hunter, R., and Sheldon, S. *Statewide Longitudinal Study (Parts I-III).* Woodland Hills, Calif.: Los Angeles Pierce College, 1980.

Quinley, J. W., and others. *One Year Later: A Follow-Up of the Harford Community College 1982 Graduates.* Bel Air, Md.: Harford Community College, 1983. (ED 237 143).

Stevenson, M. R., and Walleri, R. D. "Financial Decision Making in a Period of Retrenchment." In M. Mehallis (Ed.), *Improving Decision Making.* New Directions for Community Colleges, no. 35. San Francisco: Jossey-Bass, 1981.

*Mike Stevenson has been director of research and computing
at Mt. Hood Community College for eleven years. He is now
director of administrative systems at the University of California
at Santa Barbara.*

*R. Dan Walleri has worked in institutional research at Mt. Hood
for the last six years. He is an active member of the Association
of Institutional Research; his interests are information
technology, program evaluation, and finance.*

*Saundra M. Japely, research specialist at Mt. Hood, works with
program evaluation, student intentions, and student outcomes
information.*

The results of student outcomes studies are of little value if they are not used in institutional planning and decision making. Use of results can be made more effective if researchers understand the obstacles to information use on most college campuses and tailor their presentations to overcome them.

Increasing the Use of Student Outcomes Information

Mary K. Kinnick

Research studies on student outcomes—or on anything else—are of limited value if decision makers do not use their results. Some obstacles to effective use of study findings are a product of the fact that student outcomes research is often complex and results are rarely as precise as the kinds of information with which most college administrators routinely deal, such as enrollments and costs. Other obstacles are a product of the institutional environment—the organizational structure, the locus of the information collection function, and the orientation of top administrators toward information. Overcoming these obstacles requires researchers to be aware of the many functions that research on student outcomes can play in the decision-making process. It also requires that substantial attention be paid to developing multiple, effective methods of data presentation. The purpose of this chapter is to review institutional experience in overcoming such obstacles and to illustrate a number of information use techniques that have been successful in practice.

Most of the observations offered in this chapter are drawn from the experiences of seven institutions that were part of a national demonstration project on improving the use of outcomes information in decision making. Despite great variation among the mission and goals, leadership styles, and program mixes of these institutions, a number of factors were identified

P. T. Ewell (Ed.). *Assessing Educational Outcomes.* New Directions
for Institutional Research, no. 47. San Francisco: Jossey-Bass, September 1985.

that appear to be highly related to the use of student outcomes information. These factors are identified and discussed under two broad categories: technical and organizational. The technical category refers to qualities of the information itself. The organizational category refers to characteristics of the institution's organizational and managerial environment. Considered together, these factors can help to increase the likelihood that decision makers in colleges and universities will actually use student outcomes information.

The Multiple Roles of Student Outcomes Information

Information use can refer to more than the use of information in reaching a particular decision. Several researchers and evaluation theorists have identified the large variety of roles that information can play in decision making (Braskamp and Brown, 1980; Patton, 1978; Stufflebeam and others, 1971). Ewell and Chaffee (1984) identify four roles: identifying problems and alternatives, establishing a context for decision making, inducing action, and promoting or legitimizing action. Other, more specific applications for student outcomes information have been identified by Ewell (1983). These uses include preparing accreditation self-studies, program review, institutional planning and budgeting, and developing more effective retention and recruitment programs. Table 1 reviews some of the many roles of student outcomes information that have been identified in practice.

Within the institution itself, student outcomes information can help to identify problems, identify alternative solutions to the same problem, and make improvements in programs or changes in policy. The same information, arrayed differently or combined with other information, can also be used with external audiences, for instance, to assure state agencies, accrediting associations, legislatures, other funders, and the general public that a quality product results from support for or investment in the institution. Other roles can be played internally or externally, including providing general background information to keep individuals current on the status of the institution or justifying decisions and verifying hunches about what is actually occurring.

Obstacles to Information Use

The experiences of many institutions have helped to identify some of the obstacles that limit the use of student outcomes information. These obstacles relate primarily either to qualities of the organizational environment within which the information is developed, organized, and communicated or to qualities of the information itself and its presentation. Institutional personnel can use the list of factors summarized in Table 2 to assess the student outcomes information situation on their own campus. Each factor is discussed in the sections that follow.

Table 1. Roles of Student Outcomes Information

Internal	Internal or External	External
problem identification	general education	quality control/ accountability
solution development	action/discussion catalyst	political leverage
program improvement	decision justification	protection
policy change	verification	promotion

Table 2. Summary of Factors Affecting the Utilization of Student Outcomes Information

Technical	Organizational
readability; a focus on findings	access to the information
organizing data around problems, issues, institutional processes	organizational structure
data integrity	incentives
face validity	linkage between data users and data developers and managers
timeliness	
interpretability	
excessive bulk	lack of access
organizing reports around the data	lack of appropriate organizational structure
lack of data integrity	limited or no incentives
lack of face validity	lack of linkage between data users, developers, and managers
information arrives late	
limited interpretability	

Organizational Factors

Lack of Access to Information. Information can be inaccessible because people are not aware that it exists, because of bureaucratic red tape and internal politics, and because of the physical difficulty involved in locating and using it. One of the first steps that staff at several successful institutions have taken was to inventory student outcomes information already available and alert others to its availability. For example, Montana State University's inventory included special data bases, such as test scores and other student entry characteristics, information on student academic achievement at the university, institutional and program accreditation reports, special surveys of current student satisfaction with campus life, and numerous school- or college-maintained data bases on student progress and performance. Several other institutions have begun assessment projects by undertaking an inventory and distributing a summary report. As a result, assessment offices have received a significant number of inquiries for further information.

Bureaucratic red tape or lack of political clout can also limit access. For instance, a registrar may be authorized to approve and prioritize all requests for access to centrally controlled computerized student record files. Specific individuals may determine priorities for access to the computing resources needed to construct special reports.

Lack of an Appropriate Organizational Framework or Structure. Improving student learning and development requires the combined efforts of many offices and individuals on a campus. Unless a framework already exists for reviewing obtained information and for developing and implementing an explicit plan designed to solve identified problems, use of student outcomes data will remain limited. For example, many institutions participating in the NCHEMS/Kellogg Project created new committee structures to review data and make recommendations. Such structures were particularly useful in projects where a multifaceted campus problem, such as student retention, was under discussion.

Little or No Incentive to Use Information. For many institutions, increased use of student outcomes information may entail significant institutional change. Experiences at many institutions suggest that its use will remain limited in the absence of a formal mandate or expectation that it will be used. Examples of such a mandate or expectation include a requirement that individual departments or units include or respond to previously supplied outcomes data as part of a planning and budgeting system or as part of the self-study component of a program review process.

Lack of Linkages Between Those Who Develop, Manage, and Use Information. When the end user of the information is not linked organizationally to those who collect, maintain, and manage it, there is significantly less chance that information will be useful. At best, the resulting information will be merely interesting; at worst, it will be inaccurate. On many campuses, the registrar is responsible for student records—a rich source of student outcomes information. How such information is coded, stored, and processed has a direct bearing on the other uses to which it can be put, particularly on its uses for student retention. When the data collector or analyst does not fully understand the information needs of the end user, there is no assurance that the information will meet the user's needs. When no formal or informal linkage is in place to ensure such understanding, the potential for information use is slight.

Technical Factors

Excessive Bulk. The results of student outcomes studies are often reported in elaborate and detailed tables or narrative, and they are bound into thick reports that invite neither an initial glance nor subsequent consideration. Lengthy reports reflect an obsession for detail that tends to obscure overall findings and implications. Most administrators merely glance at such reports and file them. While they may expect to refer to them again at a later time, they rarely do.

Organizing Reports Around Data, Not Around Issues. Too many reports are data driven rather than directed toward concrete problems or established institutional processes. One major limitation of this practice is that it leaves no one on campus generally responsible for doing anything with or about the resulting information. Effective use results when information is organized around real or potential issues or problems that the institution is committed to solving. Alternatively, information is used when it is made part of ongoing institutional processes, such as planning, program review, or budgeting. Evaluation theorists (Patton, 1978; Stufflebeam and others, 1971) have noted the strong relationship between information use and the extent to which information is responsive to user needs.

Lack of Data Integrity. The term *data integrity* refers to the extent to which the data obtained are valid and reliable. At one institution, computerized data bases were constructed to produce student retention figures. The initial data proved to be inaccurate, because the data-processing procedures that were used were not the ones that project directors had asked for and that they assumed had been used. Such experiences suggest that data integrity is enhanced when those who develop, manage, and use a particular data set are formally linked within the organization and when many opportunities to detect and correct errors are built into the system.

Lack of Face Validity. The use of information is also affected by the extent to which data are perceived to be accurate. Data credibility or face validity often becomes an issue, particularly when findings are negative. At one college, open-ended comments about programs of study were solicited from students as part of a former student follow-up survey. The relatively small number of positive or negative open-ended comments made by students in particular programs were variously considered or dismissed, depending on how the comments meshed with the reviewers' picture of reality. Data users pay attention to the data that they believe are the most accurate and that tend to substantiate their own points of view.

Having Information Too Late. Too often, elaborate procedures are developed in an effort to collect the most accurate and complete information possible. When this is the case, results may not be available until long after their usefulness has peaked or interest has waned. Information may already exist that could serve at least to suggest an appropriate course of action or a further line of inquiry if it were reformatted or reanalyzed. For example, administrators at Towson State University discovered that, despite initially inaccurate attrition figures, the general pattern of results—particularly the large differences obtained between white and black students— indicated the appropriate corrective actions.

Limited Interpretability of Data. Interpretability refers to the power of data actually to inform. It depends primarily on how data are presented. For instance, if all that is known is that 30 percent of the students in a particular community college transfer to four-year institutions, what can be concluded? Is this proportion good or bad? Without some reference point, interpretation is severely limited. However, if it is also known that the figure was 42 percent five years ago and that the average for other community colleges in the state is 45 percent, the figure becomes more meaningful. If the data available are broken down by program area so that they can be compared with one another and with historical trends, they become even more meaningful. The construction of trend lines and other comparative formats can greatly enhance meaning. Such analyses place emphasis on the comparison of differences rather than on any one specific data point—a more appropriate practice when the measures used to assess outcomes are relatively imprecise, as student outcomes measures are.

Organizational Strategies: Focusing on Institutional Problems or Processes

The use of student outcomes information is greatly enhanced when the information can be incorporated into an ongoing institutional process or procedure, such as program review or strategic planning and budgeting, or when it is focused on a particular problem, such as student recruitment or retention. Such linkages can be fostered by the college or university internally, for example by administrative mandate, or by shared recognition of and concern about a current or impending crisis, such as enrollment decline, or a problem with a particular program or curriculum. Impetus may also come from outside the organization. In one case, the impetus for undertaking an analysis of student outcomes came from a consent decree between the university system and the U.S. Department of Education that stipulated increasing black enrollment in traditionally white institutions. In other cases, outcomes assessment has been linked to a state-level policy or requirement. For example, in 1979 the University of Tennessee, Knoxville, became subject to a new program of the Tennessee Higher Education Commission that allowed as much as 5 percent of an institution's annual state instructional budgetary allocation to be awarded on the basis of evidence demonstrating accomplishments on a series of performance criteria. Both external factors provided a strong incentive for data use. Several of the most common linkages between information and particular problems or processes are discussed in this section.

Focusing on Student Recruitment and Retention. Successful efforts to link outcomes information with the solution to a retention problem share several common features. Constituting new committees that brought together representatives from both the academic and student services areas was an important first step. In one case members of the committee had never before met together formally to address a common issue, and new ongoing lateral linkages across unit boundaries were forged. A second feature of successful programs was that top administration formally charged such committees with responsibility for addressing the problem and for formulating solutions. Third, in each case, top administration played a critical role in reinforcing the expectation that action steps would in fact be taken to solve the problem. In one case, an oversight committee was charged with responsibility for recommending policies to increase black student recruitment and retention by making better use of information about student behavior, achievements, and attitudes. Analysis of a large data set on admissions, enrollments, retention, and characteristics of the student experience resulted in the identification of fourteen major issues. The university's chancellor then directed administrators in each division of the university to communicate in writing what was currently being done to address the issue as well as future plans and proposed activities.

At a regional state university, a new campuswide retention committee was formed to serve as a vehicle for project development and to ensure that action steps would be taken to change the retention picture. A new mandatory advising program for freshmen and a minority mentor program resulted directly from student outcomes study findings. The existence of the campuswide committee played a particularly important role in the success of this project. The committee forged new lateral linkages among key administrators and staff members that were essential to the implementation of new programs and procedures designed to improve the retention situation.

The final example is provided by a small rural community college, which also formed a new campuswide retention committee. The committee was expected to develop and implement strategies designed to increase the persistence of specific identified student subpopulations. One major product of the effort was an early warning system that helped faculty to identify students who were in need of support service assistance, including counseling. In each of the cases just cited, the existence of a recognized campus problem helped to focus and shape the use of data.

Using Information in Program Review. A number of institutions have increased the use of research data by incorporating outcomes information into the formal academic program review process. In each case, the fundamental rationale for conducting the program review was program improvement, not cost saving. As with the retention examples, top administration in each case lent its formal support to the process and called for the formulation of program improvement plans.

An opportunity for faculty and curriculum coordinators to interact with managers and division heads about the data and its interpretation was a key component of the process at one community college. Everyone took part in a formal process that used a fourteen-factor survey instrument to develop a series of effectiveness ratings for each program. Student follow-up survey information and retention data were presented alongside other information, such as program costs and enrollments, as a basis for these ratings. The process greatly increased general understanding of the discipline area under review, the challenges that it faced, and the areas where improvement or change was needed. Numerous curricular changes resulted from this process, many of them credited to the use of the student outcomes information.

At a large research university, increased availability of outcomes information resulted in the revision of program evaluation guidelines. Previously, the guidelines had focused primarily on program input factors as evaluative criteria. The new guidelines include such factors as graduate placements, opinions concerning the quality of the program and supporting services, and achievement in general education and the major field.

Using Information in Comprehensive Planning and Budgeting. Other institutions have successfully used outcomes information in the planning and budgeting process. In one case, department heads and deans are explicitly asked to comment on selected results of student follow-up studies as part of their unit five-year plans. They review tabular summaries of information and the written comments supplied by students and former students and answer the following questions: What are the programmatic, practical, or policy implications of the data for your department, college, or school? What actions, if any, are suggested? What actions, if any, will be taken? This approach forced departments to pay attention to the student outcomes information by tying it to the established planning and resource allocation process. While responses varied by department, the general result was a heightened consciousness about improving outcomes and increased awareness that valuable information was already available.

The Special Case of Minigrants. Previous discussion suggests that the use of student outcomes information can be increased through proper use of existing incentives, such as urgent problems or required processes. Another approach is the minigrant, a bottom-up change strategy that has been used successfully in several cases.

For example, the main focus of one university's effort to use data was to offer small amounts of support to a group of competitively selected campus projects aimed at increasing access to or use of student outcomes information. Nine minigrants were awarded. The projects ranged from one that identified critical factors related to the retention and achievement of American Indian students to one that produced a videotape for use in a statewide articulation effort with secondary schools. The project encouraged broad experimentation in the use of outcomes data by individual offices and departments. As a result, the demand for further data on student outcomes and achievement increased sharply. As a by-product, linkages among the group of mid level managers who served on the project steering committee were strengthened. They have become key promoters of student outcomes information on campus and have since undertaken a number of related projects on student success.

Data Presentation Strategies

Many institutions have found that four major data presentation strategies are particularly effective in promoting the use of information: disaggregating the unit of analysis, using comparative formats, using graphics and short reports focused on a particular issue, and integrating student outcomes information with other data sets. This section illustrates these strategies.

Disaggregating the Unit of Analysis. Most successful efforts to promote the use of information have moved away from summarizing student outcomes data only for the institution or the student population as a whole. Figures 1, 2, and 3 illustrate three kinds of presentations that disaggregate data. Figure 1 presents alumni survey results comparatively by major academic division. This institution also disaggregated student outcomes data by budgetary unit as part of its planning and budgeting system.

Figure 2, taken from a community college, presents a wide variety of data about students at the most basic level of the institution, the individual course. This information is distributed each term to all course instructors. The data are also summarized by program, discipline, division, and the institution as a whole. A major concern in this effort is to provide relevant information directly to faculty—those in the most strategic position to affect the quality of the individual student's educational experience.

Figure 1. Executive Summary
May 1980 *Undergraduate* Alumni Survey

College/School:_____

	Unit Compared to Campus[a]			
	Below Average	Average	Above Average	Campus Average
I. Going to Graduate/Professional School in 1980-81:				
1. Enrolled full- or part-time[b]		37.6%		37.6%
2. Attending school of first choice		65.8%		64%
3. Department "very good" or "excellent" in preparing for grad/prof school (n = 90)		39%		44%
II. Employment in 1980-81:				
4. Employed *full-time*		58.4%		58.2%
5. Department "very good" or "excellent" in preparing student for employment (n = 96)		24%		31%
6. Median 1980-81 Salary (n = 56)	$10,999			$12,757
III. Percentage Rating Department "Very Good" or "Excellent" in:				
7. Quality of Instruction			72.3%	60%
8. Major Requirements as an Integrated Program		40%		44.3%
9. Academic Advising		27.8%		26.6%
10. Career Advising		15.8%		14.6%
11. Informal Contact with Faculty			48.5%	25.3%
IV. Percentage Who Would Attend SUNY Again		76%		74.7%

[a] Assignment to "below average," "average" or "above average" category based on test of significance (p   .10, two-tailed) of difference between unit percentage and that of all other respondents combined. When difference was non-significant, percentage was placed in "average" column.

[b] Unless noted otherwise, college/school base n = 101. Degrees awarded in May 1980 = 240. Response rate = 42%.

Office of Institutional Research, SUNY-Albany
December, 1983

Figure 2

COURSE REPORT

FOR FALL , 1983   10/ 1/1983

DIVISION: **COURSE**   DISCIPLINE:

COURSE DATA

CREDITS: 4.00   CREDIT TYPE: Transfer   GRADED/UNGRADED: Graded   RUNS 09/26 - 12/16

MEETS M W F   AT MHCC ON CAMPUS   ROOM AC 2605 0   FROM 07:40 Tu 8:50

INSTRUCTOR: INSTRUCTOR IS FULL-TIME   INSTRUCTOR'S DIVISION:

STUDENT DATA

TOTAL STUDENTS REGISTERED 38   AVERAGE AGE: 23.6   MALE/FEMALE: 19 / 19

STUDENTS RECEIVING FINANCIAL AID OR VET BENEFITS: 9   STUDENTS AUDITING COURSE: 1

AVERAGE MHCC GPA: 2 48

		5 TOF MAJORS	
Returning Students:	18	BUS NESS MGMT	7
New students:	20	GEN STUDIES/TRANSFER	4
		BUS NESS ADM N	3
		GEN STUDIES/VOCATION	3
		ADULT ENRICH	3

INTENT DATA

MOTIVE FOR ATTENDING MHCC		INTENDED MHCC DURATION		PREVIOUS EDUCATION		PRESENT EMPLOYMENT	
Getting a job	3%	1 quarter only	8%	Less than High Sch	3%	Full Time	16%
Keeping a job	3%	2 quarters	3%	GED	0%	Part Time	63%
Getting better job	13%			High School	61%		
Earn 2 year Degree	47%	1 year	26%	2yrs college, No Deg	18%	Not Employed	18%
Earn 1yr Certificate	3%	2 years	47%	3yrs or more, No Deg	5%		
Earn GED	0%			Certificate	0%		
Earn 4 year Degree	13%	3 years	3%	AA Degree	0%		
		More than 3 years	8%				
Personal Enrichment	3%			Bachelors Degree	3%		
Other	0%			Masters Deg. or PHD	3%		
No Response	0%	No Response	5%	No Response	8%	No Response	3%

Source: Office of Research, Mt. Hood Community College, Gresham, Oregon

Figure 3 is drawn from the retention program of another community college. Retention data and a broad set of information about the student body suggested that the institution was perceived and experienced quite differently by several distinct subgroups of students: full-time day transfer students, full-time day occupational students, part-time day program students, part-time evening program students, and nonprogram students. Educational goals and retention patterns were quite distinct for each group. Identification of these student prototypes enabled administrators and faculty to develop tailored, and thereby more effective, action plans to increase retention.

Using Comparative Formats and Graphics. A considerable amount of information can be conveyed comparatively and in graphic form. Figures 1, 4, and 5 provide illustrations. Figure 1, although tabular in form, allows the reviewer to scan the profile and quickly note the academic unit characteristics that fall above or below campus averages. Such pseudographic presentations can help to organize and highlight the major findings of a particular data display. The college or school unit represented in Figure 1 is above average in student ratings of the quality of instruction and informal contact with the faculty but below average in the median salary earned by alumni.

Figure 4, taken from a special report developed to inform strategies for increasing black student enrollment at a southeastern university, compares a series of admission and enrollment rates for black and white students and compares trends over a six-year period. The data may be reviewed both vertically and horizontally. Again, the table is laid out as a pseudographic. Figure 5, from another university's program review process, compares senior student responses to a question about the quality of teaching by department or program area and by college or school. The use of graphics calls attention to the departments that received ratings that were better or poorer than average. At the same time, the figure shows the variability of scores around the average attained.

Using Short, Issue-Specific Reports. One remedy to the obstacle of lengthy reports is to develop and release to specific audiences short, highly readable reports that focus on particular timely issues or problems. The more that can be placed on a single page, the better. Figures 2 and 4 illustrate the truth of this adage. Figure 3 summarizes the key information on retention and student demographics, states the retention objectives, and presents recommendations and additional observations about the student population in question—full-time day transfers—on a single page. The summary served as the focal point for development of an explicit action plan designed to increase the retention of that population.

Note that the title of Figure 4 is itself a summary statement of what the data suggest: An increasing proportion of black high school graduates are applying for admission to NCSU, and an increasing proportion of black applicants are being accepted for admission to NCSU. While this particular data display was one of many in a much larger report, each table in the report is labeled in a similar way. One by-product of this practice is that the table of contents constitutes an abstract of the report's major findings.

At another institution, information derived from a follow-up survey of graduates was used to develop short reports of approximately seven pages each. Each report related directly to a topic of general campus concern. For example, one report looks at the extent and quality of student-faculty and student-staff interactions and at the relationship between such interactions and retention and student satisfaction with the educational experience. Another provides information relating to the importance that students place on obtaining a liberal education and an appreciation of ideas—goals that the institution considers important as part of a new set of general education requirements. Reports like these provoked discussion and served to challenge some long-held myths about features of students' experience.

Integrating Outcomes Information with Other Data Sets. The value and interpretability of student outcomes information can be significantly enhanced when it is presented in combination with other information about the institution and its programs and services. Many successful institutions have followed this practice. Figures 2 and 3 illustrate such integration of data sets. One context in which such integration is particularly appropriate is program review. For example, one community college brought together a wide variety of information to support and inform a new program and discipline review process. For each of the ninety-plus disciplines identified, data on the relation between job and schooling derived from student follow-up studies were presented along with information about employment outlook (obtained from data on job market supply and demand), course retention, program and discipline completion rates, direct instructional costs, and student enrollments.

The Challenge

Patton (1978, pp. 19–20) observed that "the overall problem of under-utilization of evaluation research will not be solved by compiling and following some long list of evaluation proverbs and axioms. Real-world circumstances are too complex and unique to be routinely approached through the application of isolated pearls of evaluation wisdom." Patton's comment correctly suggests what much institutional experience has reinforced: Increasing the use of student outcomes information requires a comprehensive approach, one more organic than mechanistic in character and one that takes the local institutional context into account. Quick fix solutions that rely on laundry lists of good practices will fall short of the mark.

Figure 3. Retention Population Issue Summary

STUDENT POPULATION: Full-time Day Transfer

A. Retention Rates

	Fall 1980 Cohort	Fall 1981 Cohort
"Completers"	20.1%	24.1%
"Still Attending"	43.8%	45.4%
"First Semester Only"	20.8%	17.7%

B. Important Demographic Characteristics
55-60% male
85-90% under 20 years old
50-55% from Fulton County
15-25% "to prepare for job or career"

C. Retention Objectives/Approaches
— Increase proportion transferring to senior institutions having completed AA/AS degree
— Minimize number of students leaving for "traditional" academic or social reasons throughout the enrollment period

D. Kinds of Recommendations Needed
— Improve academic advisement on transfer requirements for senior institutions; utilize knowledge of faculty members in specific curriculum areas
— Publicize results of ICCB transfer study on value of receiving AA/AS degree in successful senior institution performance
— Maintain and improve "academic early warning system"

E. Summary
This is SRC's "traditional" college student population. Although it constitutes only about 10% of total headcount, it generates a high proportion of total FTE. Preventing *one* student from this category from leaving the institution is the equivalent in SCH terms of saving 3 part-time students. These students are likely to respond to traditional retention approaches—early warning, improved advisement, greater levels of information involvement with faculty, and other programs aimed at increasing total involvement with the institution.

Source: Spoon River College

Figure 4

An increasing proportion of black high school graduates are applying for admission to NCSU. An increasing proportion of black applicants are being accepted for admission to NCSU.

		NC HS Grads.			NCSU Applicants			NCSU Accept.			NCSU Freshman
		Number	% Apply		Number	% Accept.		Number	% Enroll		Number
1977	White	50,465	11.9%	►	6,009	70.5%	►	4,234	59.8%	►	2,532
	Black	19,727	2.9%	►	573	49.7%	►	285	56.5%	►	161
1978	White	50,440	12.7%	►	6,403	72.8%	►	4,660	57.2%	►	2,668
	Black	19,554	3.3%	►	640	58.6%	►	375	62.4%	►	234
1979	White	51,726	13.5%	►	6,976	73.1%	►	5,103	56.2%	►	2,865
	Black	19,529	4.0%	►	773	45.9%	►	355	63.9%	►	227
1980	White	50,704	13.6%	►	6,900	75.9%	►	5,237	58.5%	►	3,066
	Black	19,170	4.3%	►	828	53.1%	►	440	61.8%	►	272
1981	White	50,016	13.6%	►	6,817	64.6%	►	4,405	60.6%	►	2,668
	Black	19,188	4.9%	►	931	62.7%	►	584	56.7%	►	331
1982	White	49,904	13.7%	►	6,842	66.0%	►	4,513	60.6%	►	2,735
	Black	20,155	4.4%	►	881	63.3%	►	558	58.6%	►	327

Source: North Carolina State University

Figure 5

Senior Survey Results on Question 1-a: How do you rate the faculty in your department in the quality of their teaching?

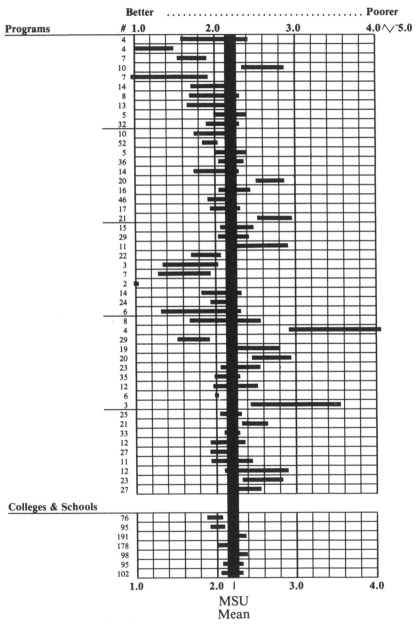

Source: Montana State University

I have suggested in this chapter that two levels of strategy are required to increase the use of student outcomes information. The first focuses directly on organizational characteristics and processes. The second focuses on characteristics and qualities of data presentation. Implementation of these strategies in combination should reduce the likelihood of the following state of affairs, which too often is the lament of higher education managers and administrators:

> Data data data. I've got data all around.
> Data in my hair. Data on the ground.
> But I ain't, I ain't got no information.
> (Kinnick, 1980)

References

Braskamp, L. A., and Brown, R. D. (Eds.). *Utilization of Evaluation Information.* New Directions for Program Evaluation, no. 5. San Francisco: Jossey-Bass, 1980.

Ewell, P. T. *Information on Student Outcomes: How to Get It and How to Use It.* Boulder, Colo.: National Center for Higher Education Management Systems, 1983.

Ewell, P. T., and Chaffee, E. E. "Promoting the Effective Use of Information in Decision Making." Paper presented at the 24th annual forum of the Association for Institutional Research, Fort Worth, Texas, May 1984.

Kinnick, M. K. "Data Data Data." Music and lyrics copyright 1980.

Patton, M. Q. *Utilization-Focused Evaluation.* Beverly Hills, Calif.: Sage, 1978.

Stufflebeam, D., and others. *Educational Evaluation and Decision Making in Education.* Itasca Ill.: Peacock, 1971.

Mary K. Kinnick is associate professor of community college education at Portland State University. She has worked extensively as a consultant to colleges and universities, and she has been active in conducting research on college students.

Successful outcomes assessment programs have many
common characteristics. Institutional researchers should
seek to recognize these signs of success and use them
as guides for developing their own campus programs.

Some Implications for Practice

Peter T. Ewell

The preceding chapters have presented many different answers to the challenge of assessing college and university outcomes. Indeed, one basic theme of this volume is that diversity is part of the nature of the enterprise, given both the range of possible outcomes that can be assessed and the many differences among educational institutions themselves. In the face of this diversity, what is the role of the institutional researcher in coordinating and implementing a campus outcomes assessment program?

The experiences of the University of Tennessee, Knoxville (UTK), Northeast Missouri State University (NMSU), and Alverno College all show that effective institutional assessment programs are team efforts. No single office or individual, no matter how well equipped, can develop such a program alone. More important, these examples stress that the involvement of many offices and individuals throughout the campus is itself beneficial. Programs are more effective and better used when clear support is available from the highest administrative levels and when all constituencies that have an interest in the information collected are included in the assessment process at every step.

Nevertheless, the independent role of the institutional researcher in stimulating, shaping, and carrying out an outcomes assessment program can be both crucial and distinctive. As Mary Kinnick emphasizes, this role

P. T. Ewell (Ed.). *Assessing Educational Outcomes.* New Directions
for Institutional Research, no. 47. San Francisco: Jossey-Bass, September 1985.

takes many forms. First, the institutional research or assessment office can serve as an important clearinghouse for existing and projected work on outcomes. As the experience of UTK and Alverno shows, one role of assessment professionals is to coordinate the work of others—often faculty—who design and conduct different parts of the assessment program. Similarly, one key role of the institutional research office in the seven NCHEMS/ Kellogg project institutions was to inventory past research on student outcomes and to let potential users know what information was available and how to use it.

Second, the institutional researcher is a technical consultant in the design of instruments and assessments and in the interpretation of data. At UTK, the project coordinator helps individual departments to construct their own senior assessment instruments when needed. At Mt. Hood Community College, institutional research staff help with the design of individual student follow-up questions or instruments in support of the program review process. Similarly, at both UTK and Alverno, one major role of assessment professionals is to interpret and discuss results (generally face-to-face) with those who have an interest in them.

Third, in many investigations of student outcomes, the institutional researcher actually conducts the research. In such areas as student tracking, the investigation of attrition, student surveys, and alumni follow-up, student outcomes assessment may already be an assigned responsibility of the institutional research office. Consequently, many institutional researchers are familiar with the rudiments of sample survey design and administration described by Endo and Bittner in Chapter Five and by Stevenson, Walleri, and Japely in Chapter Six. In such areas as student learning gain or student psychological development, outcomes assessment is generally not an assigned responsibility. In these cases, institutional researchers will need to know some of the traditions and methods described in Chapter One by Bob Pace, and they may need to become better acquainted with the kinds of instruments and approaches that Alverno currently uses. And, after the data have been collected, we can all benefit by experimenting with some of the data presentation techniques presented by Mary Kinnick in Chapter Seven.

Effective data presentation is part of the fourth and final role of the institutional researcher: that of advocate. Too often, the results of existing outcomes studies are not used because people are not aware of their existence or of their contents. At least as often, needed and wanted inquiries are not undertaken because of a general belief that the investigation of educational outcomes is impractical or excessively costly. Institutional researchers can play an important role in clarifying the concepts and methods of outcomes assessment, both existing and potential. As Trudy Banta emphasizes in her description of the UTK experience, development of an effective assessment program takes time, incentives, and the involvement of a committed group of people. Convincing faculty in particular that outcomes assessment is both feasible and beneficial will require dedication, discussion, and a great deal of listening. Institutional researchers should be ready to provide leadership in this process.

Of course, successful performance of all four roles will be for nought if top administrative support for the enterprise is lacking. Despite their diversity, one common feature of all the assessment programs described in this volume is that top administration actively sponsors and encourages them. However, few institutional researchers currently enjoy such interest and support. For many, the challenge will be to create interest and support. To meet this challenge, two strategies suggested by the preceding chapters may be of value.

First, take every opportunity to build a campus dialogue around existing student outcomes work. As Mary Kinnick describes, one theme apparent in many data utilization projects is that interest in the results of outcomes studies can be built up through short, issue-oriented, often provocative reports. As McClain and Krueger note in Chapter Three, nothing stimulates involvement better than data that appear to others to be wrong or that appear to challenge widely held beliefs and assumptions. By interacting with outcomes data, often for the first time, many potential advocates and users will become convinced of their utility. And, as the UTK experience emphasizes, this conviction can often transform an initial distaste for assessment into enthusiasm.

The second strategy is also illustrated by the UTK experience: Turn requirements into opportunities. An increasing number of external agencies, public and private, are requiring outcomes assessments from colleges and universities. Institutional responses to such requirements have varied widely. In Tennessee, many institutions treat performance funding simply as a compliance requirement and gather data accordingly. One key aspect of the UTK experience, in contrast, was that compliance was used as a way of building support for an assessment program throughout the campus community. The same process can be used in accreditation, in developing funding requests, and in a host of other externally oriented situations. For example, the new Southern Association of Colleges and Schools accreditation criteria have already stimulated several institutions in the southeast to establish outcomes assessment programs—programs advocated for many years on these campuses without result. However, as Trudy Banta notes, the key point in such situations is to keep the focus of the assessment relevant to internal concerns. External stimuli can be of enormous value in building support for outcomes assessment, but the process itself must be established by the institution, and it must serve the needs of the institution.

Given that broad campus support for outcomes assessment already exists or that it can be built, what are some of the implications of the preceding chapters for the practicing institutional researcher? Four broad lessons seem apparent, each of which recalls a familiar proverb.

Look Before You Leap

One theme of the preceding chapters is that in outcomes assessment no one starts from scratch. As Bob Pace reminds us, outcomes assessment has a long and distinguished history, and many excellent instruments and assessment models are available to the practicing researcher. Furthermore, a growing body of institutional experience in establishing programs such as those described in Chapters Two, Three, and Four is emerging. Those charged with responsibility for initiating outcomes assessment programs should take ample advantage of the fact that such tools and examples are available. Using them not only makes establishment of an institutional outcomes assessment program easier, it also generally results in better instruments and procedures, and, most important, it may allow institutions to be compared.

Furthermore, as Mary Kinnick underlines, institutional assessment projects rarely start from scratch, even if new instruments and procedures are used. One lesson of the NCHEMS/Kellogg project was that data on student outcomes usually exist in many forms at most colleges and universities—in student affairs offices, in alumni offices, and in individual departments. As a result, one of the first important steps in many successful programs is a systematic assessment and inventorying of what is already known about the impact that the institution is having on its students.

A second element of looking before you leap is also admirably illustrated by the preceding chapters: the need to plan carefully and explicitly before actually embarking on a data collection effort. Both Alverno and NMSU invested considerable time and effort in developing a conceptual scheme to guide their assessment efforts long before instruments were chosen and data were actually gathered. While UTK's effort was shaped to a large extent by the Tennessee Higher Education Commission's performance-funding criteria, it, too, benefited from extensive task force planning. And, while the experiences of the University of Colorado at Boulder and Mt. Hood were more narrowly focused, those institutions also benefited strongly from literature reviews and from the development of an explicit model to structure the enterprise.

Explicit planning is also required because successful programs are multifaceted and institutionwide efforts. The programs developed by Alverno, NMSU, and UTK all involved articulation of quite different kinds of activities—learning gain testing, psychological testing, sample surveying, and personal interviewing—undertaken by many different offices and individuals—individual faculty, departments and academic units, student service offices, central assessment offices, and external testing, evaluation, and certification agencies.

Finally, our cases illustrate the importance of actively involving a wide range of interested parties in the planning process. For Alverno, assessment remains a faculty-based and faculty-initiated activity. At UTK and NMSU, active involvement and review by all segments of the university community are important elements of the program. Finally, both Endo and Bittner and Stevenson, Walleri, and Japely remind us that involvement in the design of a particular assessment study is the only real guarantee that the results will be used effectively. In the past, too many institutional studies of student outcomes have been one-shot and acontextual. Looking before you leap serves as an important reminder that this does not have to be the case.

Make Sure the Shoe Fits

The second major theme emerging from the preceding chapters is that outcomes assessment programs need to be carefully tailored to their institutional and curricular settings. As Bob Pace emphasizes in Chapter One, there is no single right way of measuring educational outcomes, because different kinds of outcomes are the results of different educational experiences and intentions. Each of the cases presented here involves careful consideration of the match between assessment and setting. Indeed, in many cases the "best" instrument or technique was consciously not employed, because its content or coverage was inappropriate to the institution or curriculum. Finally, as Mary Kinnick notes, carefully designing the presentation of assessment results to fit the needs and experiences of particular kinds of decision makers is an important way of promoting effective use of such information.

In general, there are two distinct levels of congruence between setting and assessment design that any research project should attempt to maintain. First, the form and content of assessment should be consistent with the institution's distinctive mission and educational objectives. At Alverno, the design of assessment closely and consciously reflected that institution's concern with each student's development of generic lifelong abilities. At NMSU, the assessment effort was firmly grounded in the process of mission redefinition that resulted as the institution evolved from a teacher's college to a multipurpose, comprehensive regional university. Finally, at Mt. Hood, the decision to assess student intentions on entry as part of an outcomes research program was a result of the community college mission of service to a diverse, often occupationally oriented, student population. In each case, the design of assessment first had to confront what the institution as a whole was trying to accomplish.

Second, the tools and techniques that are used in assessment must

correspond to what is actually being taught or to what the student is actually experiencing. As Bob Pace emphasizes, it is important to continue to
ask the question, Outcomes of what? Making sure that the content of
assessments is congruent with the actual curriculum or experience is a
theme apparent at many levels. As Trudy Banta notes, much faculty concern about use of the ACT COMP instrument at UTK revolved around
whether this instrument was a good measure of general education as actually taught and intended at UTK. In the English department at NMSU,
there was concern that the GRE achievement test in that field did not
reflect the American literature emphasis of the department's undergraduate
curriculum. UTK's decision to design its own student opinion instrument
was partly the result of a review that determined that existing commercial
instruments did not adequately cover students' experience at UTK.

In addition to its impact on the choice of instruments and methodologies, the demand for specificity affects the units of analysis to be
employed. For outcomes studies, the appropriate unit of analysis is in most
cases the individual school, department, or program, not the institution
as a whole. That is the level at which student experiences actually take
place and the level with which most students actually identify. Both Kinnick and Stevenson, Walleri, and Japely cite examples of the need for sampling frames that will ensure a sufficient number of respondents for each
department. Furthermore, the individual department or unit is generally
the place where changes can be made that will make the most difference.
Excellent examples of such changes are provided by the NMSU business
college's use of ACT COMP subscores and Mt. Hood's reorientation of
several two-year occupational programs to provide more relevant, job-
specific training.

Of course, the ultimate specificity is the individual student or classroom experience. Alverno's assessment program is carefully designed to be
useful in improving individual student performance. In this sense, assessment results are part of the curriculum. At Mt. Hood, the existence of
outcomes and intentions data on the student data base allows a wide range
of computerized reports to be generated—by program, by discipline, by
instructor, or by individual class. Both instances reflect sensitivity to the
fact that different kinds of outcomes occur at different levels and that
assessment should be tailored to match the content of actual student
experience.

There Is More than One Way

The third theme emphasized by the preceding chapters is that the
best outcomes assessment programs evolve over time and involve multiple
measures of different kinds of outcomes. As both Bob Pace and Mary Kinnick remind us, the measurement of outcomes is by nature an imprecise

endeavor, even if we know exactly which dimensions to assess. Examining student development over time is simply not like counting students, calculating loads, or many of the other more traditional activities of the institutional researcher. The analyst needs to live with greater error components and make do with less precise procedures. The answer to this difficulty, as shown by practice in the cases before us, lies in a combination of methods.

The best assessment processes employ multiple measurement criteria and techniques. At UTK, NMSU, and Alverno, many different kinds of outcomes are assessed: general cognitive skills, discipline-related knowledge and skills, and indiviual attitudes and satisfactions. Moreover, at Alverno, this aproach is an explicit design principle of assessment and evaluation; the triangulated design reported by Mentkowski and Loacker ensures methodological redundancy in both instruments and levels of analysis. In an area that by its nature is imprecise, such approaches help to ensure that what is being measured is real, not an artifact of a particular approach or measurement procedure.

A second way of overcoming the measurement difficulty is to try out different interpretations or levels of confidence on the data obtained. As Kinnick notes, the most effective presentations of outcomes data are generally comparative, displaying results of similar assessments over time, across units, or across institutions. Such presentations focus attention on the differences between the results obtained from different populations, not on the magnitude of the results themselves. Furthermore, as Endo and Bittner note, assessments based on sample surveys must always be checked for bias, and the results must be adjusted accordingly. In both cases, analysis requires sensitivity in interpretation, and it requires viewing the data from more than one perspective.

The counterpart of multiple measurement procedures is the use of multiple data presentation strategies. As Kinnick reports, one major lesson from the NCHEMS/Kellogg project is that the results of outcomes studies should address multiple issues and be tailored to multiple audiences; the same report will not work for everyone. Furthermore, the most effective presentations make use of a variety of techniques, often a mixture of text, graphics, and numerical tables. Indeed, the objective of many of the presentation techniques illustrated by Kinnick is to engage the user in a dialogue with the data. The object of analysis is less to provide answers than to present a framework within which the proper questions can be asked.

This leads to my last point about methodological multiplicity: the fact that different perspectives can be immensely valuable in the interpretation of data on outcomes. The importance of broad involvement in the designing of outcomes studies has already been mentioned. Broad involvement in drawing their implications is equally important. Many successful institutional programs use campuswide committees to interpret data;

involvement of different perspectives often leads to new insights on student perceptions and achievements. At Alverno and NMSU, results of institutionwide evaluation and assessment are publicly discussed, and collective strategies are developed. At UTK, results of department-specific assessments are discussed face-to-face among researchers and members of the department. In all cases, the existence of multiple perspectives has enabled much more comprehensive recommendations and actions to be undertaken.

The Object Is to Learn

In Chapter One, Bob Pace notes that evaluation, instruction, and feedback are all part of the same theme and that this theme is as applicable to institutional learning as it is to individual learning. All the cases presented in this volume show that improvements in student learning partly depend on our learning more about ourselves and about the institutions that we inhabit. Thus, the final lesson for practitioners is that improvements in teaching and learning and in the environment within which they take place are the ultimate objectives of outcomes studies.

This lesson has many referents. First, it refers to individual institutional research practitioners. As all the contributers to this volume remark, the act of constructing and refining an institution-specific outcomes research program is itself an ongoing learning experience. New refinements are continually added, new approaches are tried, and new interpretations of existing data are discussed. Indeed, one of the major attractions of outcomes research is its continuously developmental quality. As a result, the most successful practitioners have remained open to comment, discussion, and criticism. Like any learning process, effective studies are a collective product.

Second, learning applies to colleges and universities as institutions. To be effective, outcomes assessment demands that an educational community pay more than usual attention to careful definition of its educational objectives. In the course of stating such objectives, the community as a whole becomes more conscious collectively of what it is about, of how it is doing, and of how it can improve. This kind of attention is an important step in the attainment and maintenance of quality in an undergraduate instructional program.

Finally, of course, learning applies to the ultimate object of the enterprise: individual students in individual classrooms. If outcomes studies, or anything else that colleges and universities do, are to be counted as effective, the results must be apparent here. The ultimate implication for research practitioners is thus a simple one: Any proposed research program must successfully pose and answer the question of how the resulting information can be used to improve student experience or performance. The answer may be indirect. It will certainly depend on many circumstances outside the researcher's control. But, the question must always be present.

Peter T. Ewell is a senior associate at the National Center for Higher Education Management Systems (NCHEMS). He directs the NCHEMS/Kellogg Student Outcomes Project.

Some common sources of student outcomes information.

Appendix

Peter T. Ewell

Many instruments and procedures for the assessment of student learning and development are currently available. This appendix describes some of the most widely available and commonly used tests and questionnaires. Those who are beginning to construct a campus assessment program can use it as a starting point, but it is by no means a place to finish. Individual items are grouped according to major outcomes assessment headings.

General Knowledge

As noted in Chapter One, many tests of general knowledge have been developed over the years. Descriptions of four of the most commonly used follow.

The American College Testing (ACT) Program College Outcomes Measure Project (COMP) (source: American College Testing Program, Iowa City, Iowa) is designed to measure the general knowledge and skills presumed to be outcomes of undergraduate education. It consists of three instruments for assessing six areas of general knowledge: an objective test, an activity inventory, and a composite examination. Scoring is done by faculty trained by ACT personnel.

The Graduate Record Examination (GRE) General Examinations (source: Educational Testing Service, Princeton, New Jersey) are designed to measure undergraduate students' verbal and mathematical aptitude for

P. T. Ewell (Ed.). *Assessing Educational Outcomes.* New Directions
for Institutional Research, no. 47. San Francisco: Jossey-Bass, September 1985.

graduate work. The tests are normed against graduate school–bound students. Subscores and item analyses are not currently available.

The ACT College Admissions Test (source: American College Testing Program, Iowa City, Iowa) is designed to be used as an undergraduate admissions test, but it is suitable for administration or readministration to current college students. It covers four broad subject areas: English, math, science, and social science. Subscores and item analyses are available.

The Undergraduate Assessment Program (UAP) (source: Educational Testing Service, Princeton, New Jersey) is designed to assess the student's level of achievement at the end of an undergraduate program. It has three area components: humanities, science, and social science. It is no longer offered regularly by the ETS.

Knowledge in Particular Fields

Many standardized tests are available for assessing performance in specific fields. They include both tests of particular academic disciplines and tests designed to measure aptitude or performance in particular occupations or professions, such as law, business, or nursing. The most commonly used college-level field examinations are described here.

The Graduate Record Examination (GRE) Field Examinations (source: Educational Testing Service, Princeton, New Jersey) are designed to assess acquired knowledge of specific academic disciplines. Thirty field examinations are currently available. Item and subscore analyses are not available.

The College-Level Examination Program (CLEP) (source: The College Board, New York, New York) is designed to assess achievement or mastery of particular bodies of knowledge covered by college courses or sequences of courses. There are approximately forty-five tests in the current inventory. Consulting services on test evaluation are available.

Attitudes and Satisfaction of Students and Former Students

Many institutions have designed their own survey instruments to assess the opinions of currently enrolled students, alumni, and former students. Standardized instruments have the virtue of allowing limited interinstitutional comparison, and many are supported by a data analysis service and consultation that can help users to interpret results. Five of the most common such instruments are described in this section.

The ACT Evaluation Survey Service (ESS) (source: American College Testing Program, Iowa City, Iowa) is designed to assess student attitudes, perceptions of growth, and subsequent educational and occupational experiences at different points of the student's college career. It includes survey questionnaires for current students, former students, and alumni.

A computer data analysis service is available. Comparative data from other institutions that use the service are available by type of institution. Additional local questions may be added to the standardized questionnaires.

The NCHEMS/College Board Student Outcomes Information Service (SOIS) (source: National Center for Higher Education Management Systems, Boulder, Colorado) is designed to assess student attitudes, perceptions of growth, and subsequent educational and employment experience at different points of the student's college career. Evaluations of specific college services are included. It contains six questionnaires in two-year and four-year versions for new students, current students, former students, and alumni. A computer data analysis service is available. Comparative data from other institutions using the service are available by type of institution. Additional local questions may be added to the standardized questionnaires.

The Pace College Student Experiences Questionnaire (CSEQ) (source: Higher Education Research Institute, University of California, Los Angeles) is designed to measure quality of student effort in college. It contains fourteen scales or measures on the use of college facilities and opportunities for learning and development and eight scales or measures on student assessment of the college environment. Computer analysis and consulting on data interpretation are available.

The Cooperative Institutional Research Program (CIRP) (source: Cooperative Institutional Research Program, University of California, Los Angeles) is designed for use in value-added research. It contains a wide variety of student goals and general attitudinal items for entering and continuing students. Comparative data across years are available. National norms are published by type of institution.

The TEX-SIS Follow-Up System (source: Tarrant County Junior College District, Fort Worth, Texas) is designed explicitly for community and two year colleges. Designed primarily to assess occupational, employment, and continuing education outcomes, it includes seven postcard-sized questionnaire instruments for new students, current students, dropouts, graduates, and employers of graduates. It was designed explicitly to maximize mailed survey response rates.

Additional Sources

Many individual student assessment and evaluation instruments have been created by particular campuses for their own purposes. Here are four of the more useful collections of such materials:

Alverno College Research Reports (source: Alverno Productions Publications, Alverno College, Milwaukee, Wisconsin) are available for purchase on many aspects of Alverno's assessment and evaluation programs. These reports document the particular instruments used to examine different kinds of student values and abilities.

A book entitled *Surveying Your Alumni* by Barbara McKenna (source: Council of Independent Colleges, Washington, D.C.) contains twenty-two documented examples of alumni surveys successfully employed by private colleges.

The CIC Planning Data System (PDS) (source: Council of Independent Colleges, Washington, D.C.) is a collection of eleven "modules" for collecting different kinds of planning information. Designed for small independent colleges, it includes instruments on student experiences, activities, recruitment, campus goals and climate, and outcomes.

The California Community Colleges FIPSE Project on Learner Outcomes (source: Chancellor's Office, California Community Colleges, Sacramento) is a three-year project. It has produced two documents of interest to community colleges: An item bank contains more than 500 questionnaire items on a variety of topics, and a handbook on learner outcomes data reviews many locally available sources of data on assessing student learning.

Peter T. Ewell is a senior associate at the National Center for Higher Education Management Systems (NCHEMS). He directs the NCHEMS/Kellogg Student Outcomes Project.

Index

A

Achievement tests: nationally normed, 8–10; outcomes assessment with, 8–10, 21, 26–27, 121–122; task force selection of, 21–22
Alexander, 7, 11, 17
Alexander, L., 30
Alumni, outcomes assessment of, 14–15
Alverno College: elements of success at, 111, 112, 114, 115, 117, 118; instruments from, 123; validating outcomes assessment at, 47–64
American Association of State Colleges and Universities, 34
American College Testing (ACT) Program, 9, 20, 21, 25, 26, 27, 36, 38, 40–42, 68, 61, 78, 84, 116, 121, 122; Evaluation Survey Service of, 13, 71, 122–123; Opinion Survey of, 22. *See also* College Outcomes Measures Project
American Institute of Certeified Public Accountants (AICPA), Level II Achievement Exam of, 36, 38, 43
Antioch University, local assessment at, 12
Aristotle, 7, 11, 17
Astin, A. W., 37, 46, 68, 71, 78
Austin, G. R., 44, 46

B

Banta, T. W., 4, 19–32, 112, 113, 116
Benedict, L., 86n, 112, 115, 117
Bittner, I., 4, 65–79, 12, 15, 17
Braskamp, L. A., 94, 109
Brown, R. D., 94, 109

C

California Community Colleges, 124
California Longitudinal Study, 90
Centers of Excellence (Tennessee), 30
Chaffee, E. E., 94, 109
Chicago, University of, local assessment at, 12

Chicago City Junior College, local assessment at, 12
College Admissions Test, 122
College Board, 8, 9, 22, 68, 71, 84, 122, 123
College-Level Examination Program (CLEP), 8–9, 122
College Outcomes Measures Project (COMP), 9, 20, 21, 24, 25, 26–27, 29, 36, 38, 116, 121
College Student Experiences Questionnaire (CSEQ), 123
Colorado at Boulder, University of: elements of success at, 114; longitudinal data file at, 65–79
Communication, for outcomes assessment, 31
Cooperative Institutional Research Program (CIRP), 22, 68, 71, 123
Cooperative Study of Evluation in General Education, 10
Cooperative Test Service, 8
Council of Independent Colleges (CIC), 124
Critical Thinking Appraisal, 60
Cromwell, L., 63

D

Datta, L., 82, 91
Defining Issues Test, 60
Dembowski, F. L., 67, 78
Dennison, J. D., 90, 91
Dillman, D. A., 71, 77, 78, 86, 87, 91
Dissemination, of outcomes assessment results, 23–24
Doherty, A., 48, 52, 53, 58, 63
Drake University, local assessment at, 12
Dressel, P., 10, 16, 18

E

Early, M., 48, 53
Educational Testing Service (ETS), 8, 9, 10, 121, 122. *See also* Undergraduate Assessment Program

Endo, J., 4, 65–79, 112, 115, 117
Engineer-in-Training exam, 22
Enthoven, A. C., 39, 46
Ewell, P. T., 1–5, 68, 71, 78, 94, 109, 111–119, 121–124

F

Feldman, K. A., 67, 78
Fey, J., 63
Florida, academic skills test in, 2
Florida, University of, local assessment at, 12
Follow-up studies: analysis of, 81–91; analyzing and presenting results of, 88–90; changing nature of, 90; and confidentiality, 85; data collection for, 85–86; data compilation for, 88; instrument for, 84–85; maximizing response rate for, 87–88; procedures for, 85–88; program-level results from, 84; purposes of, 82; support and involvement for, 83; survey population for, 83–84; survey structure for, 83–84; timing of, 84; tracking responses in, 86–87; uses of, 89–90
Forrest, A., 21, 27, 31
Friedlander, J., 82, 91
Fund for the Improvement of Postsecondary Education (FIPSE), Project on Learner Outcomes of, 124

G

Gaff, J. G., 67, 78
Garber, H., 44, 46
General education, achievement in, 21, 26–27, 121–122
Glaser, E., 58, 60, 64
Graduate Record Examination (GRE), 8, 9, 21, 27, 36, 38, 116, 121, 122
Graduating Student Questionnaire (GSQ), 36, 43

H

Harris, C. W., 78
Heist, P., 11, 18
Higher Education Research Institute, 123
Holland, J., 11, 18
Hunter, R., 90, 91

I

Institutional researcher, roles of, 111–113

Institutional Student Survey (ISS), 36
Interests, values, and personality traits, measures of, 10–11

J

Japely, S. M., 4–5, 81–91, 112, 115, 116

K

Kellogg Foundation, 20, 31, 96, 112, 114, 117
King, M. R., 78
Kinnick, M. K., 5, 93–109, 111, 112, 113, 114, 115, 116, 117
Klemp, G., Jr., 59, 63
Kohlberg, L., 58, 60, 63
Krueger, D. W., 4, 33–46, 113

L

Lacy, W. B., 67, 79
Law School Admission Test, 45
Lay, R., 67, 79
Leadership, for outcomes assessment, 24–26, 30
Lee, Y. S., 79
Lenning, O. T., 67, 79
Litten, L. H., 67, 79
Loacker, G., 4, 47–64, 117
Loevinger, J., 58, 60, 63
Longitudinal data file: analysis design for, 74; analysis of, 65–79; background on, 65–66; building, 72–74; concerns about, 73; constructing, 73–74; data analysis for, 75; data sources for, 68–72; designing, 66–72; interpreting findings from, 75–76; presenting information from, 76–77; recommendations for, 77–78; and student characteristics, 74–75; student cohort for, 68; studies using, 74–76; variables selected for, 66–68

M

McBer and Company, 21, 60
McClain, C. J., 4, 33–46, 113
McClelland, D., 32, 59, 60, 63, 64
McKenna, B., 124
Maguire, J. J., 67, 79
Major field, achievement in, 21–22, 27–28, 122
Mayhew, L., 10, 16, 18
Medical College Admission Test, 45
Mentkowski, M., 4, 47–64, 117
Messick, S., 60, 64

Micek, S. S., 79

Michigan State University, local assessment at, 12

Middle States Association of Colleges and Schools, 2

Mines, R., 60, 64

Minnesota, University of, General College assessments at, 12

Mississippi, outcomes assessment in, 2

Missouri: Department of Higher Education in, 43; outcomes assessment in, 2, 33–46

Moeser, M., 64

Montana State University, utilization at, 96, 108

Mt. Hood Community College (MHCC): elements of success at, 112, 114, 115, 116; follow-up studies at, 81–91; utilization at, 103

N

National Center for Higher Education Management Systems (NCHEMS), 20, 22, 31, 38, 67, 68, 71, 84, 96, 112, 114, 117, 123

National Institute of Education (NIE), 53; Study Group on the Conditions of Excellence in American Higher Education of, 1, 2, 5

National Teacher Examination (NTE), 36, 38

Newcomb, T. M., 67, 78

North Carolina State University, utilization at, 104–105, 107

North Central Association of Colleges and Schools, 2

Northeast Missouri State University (NMSU): elements of success at, 111, 114, 115, 116, 117, 118; outcomes assessment at, 33–46

O

Omnibus Personality Inventory, 11

Opinions measures, for outcomes assessment, 22–23, 28–30, 122–123

Oregon: Department of Education in, 89; follow-up studies in, 82, 83

Outcomes assessment: with achievement tests, 8–10, 21, 26–27, 121–122; of alumni, 14–15; analysis of, 7–18; analysis of programs of, 19–32; assumptions and components of, 48–50, 53–55; benefits of, 2, 52–53, 61–62; case study of, 33–46; characteristics of, 50–52, 59–61, 111–119; communication for, 31; components of, 55–59; concluding observations on, 16–18; creating support for, 113–114; and culminating activities, 23; across curriculum, 53–62; data analysis for, 38–39; data elements in, 37–38; demand for, 1–3; design of, 20–23, 34–37; dissemination for, 23–24; by expert observers, 11; with follow-up studies, 81–91; future of, 44–45; holistic focus on, 51–52; implications of, 30–31; of individual student performance, 48–53; of interests, values, and personality traits, 10–11; leadership for, 24–26, 30; and learning, 118; local, 11–12, 123–124; longitudinal, 15–16, 65–79; in major field, 21–22, 27–28, 122; multiplicity in, 56–59, 116–118; opinions measures for, 22–23, 28–30, 122–123; planning for, 114–115; problems with, 15–16; recommendations on, 45–46; responsibility for, 52; results of, 62–63; roles of, 94, 95; sources on, 121–124; from student reports, 12–14; as tailored to setting, 115–116; technical support for, 30–31; time for, 31; types of, 3–4; uses of, 26–30, 39–44; utilization of, 93–109; validating, 47–64; value-added model of, 37, 45

P

Pace, C. R., 4, 7–18, 22, 67, 79, 112, 114, 115, 116, 118, 123

Pascarella, E. T., 67, 79

Patton, M. Q., 94, 97, 105, 109

Pennsylvania College for Women, local assessment at, 12

Perry, W., Jr., 58, 60, 64

Piaget, J., 58, 64

Planning Data System (PDS), 124

Popham, W., 56, 64

Purdue University, School of Science assessment at, 12

Q

Quinley, J. W., 87, 91

R

Rest, J., 58, 60, 64

Richardson, G. T., 78

Rokeach, M., 11, 18
Rossi, P., 60, 64
Rutherford, D., 63

S

San Francisco State University, local assessment at, 12
Schafer, J., 63
Sentence Completion Test, 60
Service, A. L., 79
Sequential Tests of Educational Progress, 38
Sheldon, S., 90, 91
South Dakota, outcomes assessment in, 2
Southern Association of Colleges and Schools, 2, 113
Spoon River College, utilization at, 106
State University of New York at Albany, utilization at, 102
Stephens College, local assessment at, 12
Stevenson, M. R., 4-5, 81-91, 112, 115, 116
Stewart, A., 32, 64
Strait, M., 64
Student Outcomes Information Service (SOIS), 22, 71, 123
Student Satisfaction Survey (SSS), 22-23, 24, 28-29
Stufflebeam, D., 94, 97, 109
Syracuse University, local assessments at, 12

T

Tarrant County Junior College District, 123
Tennessee, Knoxville, University of (UTK): elements of success at, 111, 112, 113, 114, 115, 116, 117, 118; outcomes assessment program at, 19-32, 99
Tennessee Higher Education Commission (THEC), 1-2, 19-20, 21, 31, 32, 99, 114
Terenzini, P. T., 67, 79

Terminal and Instrumental Values Scales, 11
TEX-SIS Follow-Up System, 123
Thrash, P., 2, 5
Tinto, V., 67, 79
Towson State University, utilization at, 98

U

Undergraduate Assessment Program (UAP), 8, 27, 36, 38, 43, 122
U.S. Department of Education, 99
Utilization: and access to information, 96; analysis of, 93-109; and bulk of reports, 97; challenge for, 105, 109; and data integrity, 97; and data set integration, 105; and disaggregation, 101, 104; and face validity, 97-98; formats and graphics for, 104; incentives for, 96; and interpretability, 98; nd issues orientation, 97, 104-105; linkages for, 96-97; minigrants for, 101; obstacles to, 94-98; organizational factors in, 96-97, 98-101; organizational structure for, 96; in planning and budgeting, 100-101; in program review, 100; for recruitment and retention, 99-100; technical factors in, 97-98, 101-105; and timeliness, 98

V

Validity, design- and performance-based, 55
Vocational Education Act, 82
Vocational Preference Inventory, 11

W

Walleri, R. D., 4-5, 81-91, 112, 115, 116
Watson, G., 58, 60, 64
Weiss, C., 60, 64
Western Washington College of Education, local assessment at, 12
Winter, D., 21, 32, 58, 60, 64

Y

Yonge, G., 11, 18